RISING WITH HOPE

Books by Mark Chironna

On the Edge of Hope
Rising with Hope

A 30-DAY DEVOTIONAL
for OVERCOMING ANXIETY
and DEPRESSION

MARK CHIRONNA

a division of Baker Publishing Group
Minneapolis, Minnesota

Published by Chosen Books
Minneapolis, Minnesota
ChosenBooks.com

Chosen Books is a division of
Baker Publishing Group, Grand Rapids, Michigan

Printed in the United States of America

Library of Congress Cataloging-in-Publication Data

Names: Chironna, Mark, author.
Title: Rising with hope : a 30-day devotional for overcoming anxiety and depression / Mark Chironna.
Description: Minneapolis, Minnesota : Chosen, a division of Baker Publishing Group, [2024] | Includes bibliographical references.
Identifiers: LCCN 2023050916 | ISBN 9780800772932 (paper) | ISBN 9780800772956 (casebound) | ISBN 9781493445660 (ebook)
Subjects: LCSH: Anxiety—Religious aspects—Christianity. | Suffering—Religious aspects—Christianity. | Hope—Religious aspects—Christianity. | Devotional calendars.
Classification: LCC BV4908.5 .C397 2024 | DDC 242/.4—dc23/eng/20240105
LC record available at https://lccn.loc.gov/2023050916

Cover design by Studio Gearbox

Baker Publishing Group publications use paper produced from sustainable forestry practices and postconsumer waste whenever possible.

24 25 26 27 28 29 30 7 6 5 4 3 2 1

To my grandchildren—
Ariana, Mark, Londyn, and Enzo:
I love you more each day.

By Grace I Endure

In the crucible of profound suffering, life
stretches into an eternal moment,
An existence under siege, where every
breath is an act of defiance,
Haunted by a relentless shadow, a
depression that hangs heavy,
An anxiety that winds its icy fingers around
my heart, squeezing till it feels ready to burst.

Sleep, a promised refuge, betrays, morphing
into a cruel illusion,
The nights spent in a deafening silence, a
stage for my restless mind,
Haunted by the ghost of peace, a specter
fading with each passing second,
Every tick of the clock a reminder of the
battle that rages in the solitude.

Pain, an uninvited guest, sets up residence,
its weight unbearable,
A desire to shed the skin, to escape the
prison of tormenting sensations,
Yet held captive in my own flesh, where
suffering paints its masterpiece,
A portrait of a soul in turmoil, an
embodiment of enduring.

It's a storm that swallows the horizon,
turning day into an endless night,
The familiar morphs into a threatening
landscape, hope seems a foreign language,
Yet clung to every moment is a desperate
hope, a life raft in a sea of despair,
A testament to the tenacity of my spirit,
hope against hope, a beacon in the storm.

When the season shifts, it is not with the
fanfare of victory,
But with the quiet humility of a survivor
taking my first step into a new dawn,
Emerging from the shadow not with a leap,
but a gentle stride,
A slow unwinding from the night, a testament
to a strength discovered in the depths.

For in the heart of the storm, in the grip of
despair,
Grace weaves its quiet magic, a thread that
holds when all else gives way,
From the ashes of a life upended, arises a
phoenix, testament to survival,
A silent proclamation, that even in the face
of life's storms, by grace, I endure.

CONTENTS

INTRODUCTION

As I pen these words, we have entered the Lenten season, the sacred calendar's reminder that we are ever moving toward the fullness of redemption. Whatever the season, I never tire of celebrating Christ's resurrection, even as I realize that His sufferings were quite dark. What God accomplished in that darkness reaches beyond our conscious grasp and overcomes our sinful human condition and the death that held its grip on us all.

Mark's gospel tells us, "When it was noon, darkness came over the whole land until three in the afternoon. At three o'clock Jesus cried out with a loud voice, 'Eloi, Eloi, lema sabachthani?' which means, 'My God, my God, why have you forsaken me?'" (Mark 15:33–34). The text describes a three-hour darkness not unlike the three-day plague of darkness that fell on Egypt (see Exodus 10:21–29).

Does that scene remind you of a dark time in your life, maybe even your current season? Do you feel stuck in a position that you cannot escape? Are you intensely anxious because you feel yourself being stretched in every direction?

Think about any deep-seated fears that may be nagging at you. Do you sense a deep dread as though your life were hanging in the balance? And amid all of that, does it seem that God is nowhere to be found?

Jesus experienced all of that on Good Friday. If we live long enough, you and I will face similar experiences. Once He bent His knees to pray in Gethsemane, Jesus entered our existential dread and anxiety and faced the intense agony of our primal fears. He sweat drops of blood as He allowed the agony to overtake Him. Terrible as it was, *it was the beginning of our deliverance from sin and death*. Jesus collapsed under the weight of our human darkness, yet He arose from prayer devoted to the will of God, knowing that the Father would glorify Him because of His self-sacrificial, self-emptying love.

Our seasons of suffering are not as intense as what Jesus endured. Yet we can feel overwhelmed and powerless in the presence of our primal fears and the dread of not knowing what's next or whether even more pain awaits us around the corner. We can know this, however: Our trouble will not last forever, as this devotional will show. It is designed to move you through the "My God, my God, why?" experiences, reassuring you that your present season is not a life sentence.

Dante Alighieri (1265–1321 CE) wrote one of the greatest classical pieces of literature of all time, and its significance endures to this day. I mention it for a reason. *Divine Comedy* is in three parts, beginning with *Inferno*, the journey through hell that started on Good Friday. Dante opens his journey to Sheol this way:

> In the middle of the journey of our life, I came to myself, in a dark wood, where the direct way was lost. It is a hard thing to speak of, how wild, harsh, and impenetrable that wood was, so that thinking of it recreates the fear. It is scarcely less bitter than death: but, in order to tell of the good that I found there, I must tell of the other things I saw there.[1]

I want to remind you of the dream I shared in the epilogue of *On the Edge of Hope*. The dream occurred at the very beginning of the three-and-a-half-year dark season the book describes. For sixteen years now, I have lived with that dream, reflecting on it again and again. I relate it to Dante's words, because I felt as though hell itself had swallowed me up. I wasn't at midlife as Dante was. But I was in the middle of a season when I thought that anything I could ever want was being made possible for me—until I reached my "dark wood." Ultimately, that crisis—the most intense of any I have ever faced—became my life's midpoint. Since then, I speak of my journey in terms of "before" or "after" my dark season.

Such seasons tend to surprise us. Dante describes a place that seemed haunted, a place he did not expect to encounter when he did. He was "off the beaten path," with no GPS and no sense of how to move forward. In the language of one psycholinguistic expert, Dante was in a territory without maps,[2] a place he found hard to articulate. I get it—I've been there! Talk about a place that is "wild, harsh, and impenetrable"! That is where I was—and where you might be now.

When Dante talked about his experience afterward, he felt all the fears all over again. When Chosen Books asked me to write about my "dark wood" encounter, it was fifteen years after the fact. I indeed felt those fears all over again, but from a different place of understanding them. I can relate to Dante's "scarcely less bitter than death" comment, yet like him, I found good in my dark season! That was the reason I wrote the book, and it's why I am writing this devotional.

God directs our paths even when we are not as conscious of our reality as we might be. Often, more things are happening of which we are *un*aware because we are not conscious of them. Until something significant happens—a dark wood of some kind—we remain "asleep." Then, when we least expect it, the darkness awakens us, and we realize our need to become more fully and consciously attuned.

The resemblance between Dante's intro to his *Inferno* and the beginning of my dark season grips me for many reasons, not the least of which is the dream that launched my trial. In that dream, I faced an open door leading from the basement of my grandparents' home to a dark-wooded, dark-clouded ancient graveyard somewhere in Europe. As dreams do, this one enabled me to see and do things that would be impossible in waking life. There was no lower-level basement door leading to the outdoors from my grandparents' actual home. And no such door could have led me into medieval Europe, before an ancient grave with a huge granite Celtic cross that was green with oxidation on one side.

From where I stood, I saw tree roots forcing the left-hand corner of the cross upward at an angle. (There are so many significant metaphors from my unconscious here!) As I stood there, I felt a heavy sense of dread and terror, but also awe and reverence. Something significant was in the atmosphere as I stood on holy ground, terrified. I think it must have been that way for the children of Israel as they stood below Mount Sinai, the entire mountain surrounded by dark clouds and seemingly ablaze as the ground shook and they trembled (see Exodus 19:16–25).

At the time of my graveyard dream, I had little or no awareness of what the dream was trying to tell me. I understand much more of it now. I was having a numinous encounter, an experience with the holy, sacred, and mysterious otherness that defies logical explanation. All you can do in such moments is say, "Woe is me, for I am undone!" (Isaiah 6:5 NKJV). The encounter affected me spiritually and psychologically. I was profoundly aware of being unaware, specifically of how much I did not know but needed to know.

I was in a dark place—my own internal basement hidden under layers of conscious awareness. It was the realm of things stored so deep that I was unconscious of them. The house was familiar enough because I had grown up in it. But now the house was deep inside me. It was my internal home where the things I had long forgotten remained unconsciously alive and present. They were tied to fears of death and of the unknown dark places that were represented by barren, somber trees and the ancient gravestone.

I was reminded that the ancient Celtic Christians were powerful missionaries living in a challenging era of persecution and violence. Even in the toughest places, they managed to preach the gospel and operate in signs and wonders. I knew the gravestone attested to someone's testimony in

Christ Jesus during a difficult time in history. The thought arrested me! I felt a little like Ebeneezer Scrooge at his burial plot, begging the Ghost of Christmas Yet to Come to give him another chance at life.

In my dream, the heavy granite gravestone sitting atop the remains of a former saint had been there so long that the roots of a huge tree now partially dislodged it. The site was weathered, in need of attention and care. I didn't realize it at the time, but the dream was telling me something about myself and about the attention and care I would need, not only to weather the hard season ahead but to be healed.

Please let this devotional take you on a journey to reveal what might be buried below the levels of your conscious awareness. Let it take you to the place where Christ's death and life are continually being applied to any unfinished business that needs your attention. I trust that the dark wood depicted by my dream will be a metaphor for the journey back from the grave to newness of life in the resurrected Jesus. May you encounter His numinous presence as you pray through this little book.

Firmly on the Edge of Hope

The Lord is my shepherd; I shall not want. He makes me lie down in green pastures; he leads me beside still waters; he restores my soul. He leads me in right paths for his name's sake. Even though I walk through the darkest valley, I fear no evil, for you are with me.

Psalm 23:1–4

Thoughts of Hope

Beloved, the last place you or I would choose to visit is what David called "the darkest valley." Like Dante's dark wood or the graveyard I visited in my dream, such places are probably not among your most desired destinations. Nevertheless, God's chosen king went there. In fact, the Scriptures reveal he visited the place more than once.

Like it or not, you visit it, too. You might be there now, crying out to God and begging Him to lead you out of your "bad dream." I don't know what kind of anguish you are facing, but I know the mark it leaves. I know how it feels to be trapped in a situation without exits, a place where relief seems nonexistent and the pain seems too great to bear. You try to fix whatever is broken, only to realize that you cannot fix yourself. Your only hope is that your Shepherd will say, "Pack your bags! We're heading back to those green pastures I told you about."

Having lived a little and pastored for many years, I know that when you want out of a dark season, you can misunderstand what is happening there. Pain is disorienting. Explaining your pain is difficult, and processing it is even harder. What you believe about suffering can also complicate matters. You may have heard a sermon about how Christians should never suffer. Maybe a friend told you that sickness and sorrow are signs of weak faith.

Nobody wants to admit they are suffering with that kind of condemnation coming at them. Crossing your dark valley is hard enough; being accused of faithlessness is an added burden you don't want or need. For the record, all people suffer. If suffering were a sign of weak faith, David would never have suffered. He was a man of great faith—not a perfect man, but a man who believed God.

Of course, there is another reason we don't acknowledge our dark woods: We feel unable to make sense of them. They are confusing, and they reveal how much we don't know about ourselves and our struggles. That is how it was in my dream. I knew I was terrified, but the reason escaped me. I had buried experiences so deep in my unconscious mind that I lost sight of them.[1] I could not acknowledge what was buried because I did not know I had buried it!

Sometimes you cannot see what you covered over until a crisis forces it back to the surface. Then you cannot unsee it. It doesn't matter who you are or what you do. Even if you spend your life helping others, you are not exempt from the kind of suffering that seems to come out of nowhere. You might feel, as I did, like you have been hit by a bus. If you had seen that bus coming, you would have jumped out of the way. But you didn't see it, at least not consciously. You did not notice the storm that was brewing, so you did what most of us do when we are in the dark about ourselves, our wellness, and the issue of suffering—you put one foot in front of the other and kept going.

Being human, I know how that works. I have been there, done that, and bought all the T-shirts. The good news is that, regardless of what you do or do not know, you are firmly planted on the edge of hope. Why? Because the all-knowing God is gracious and merciful and continually invites you to rediscover the parts of yourself you tucked away. He will not leave you to navigate your dark valleys alone. Your Shepherd is "the God of hope" who fills you "with all joy and peace in believing, so that you may abound in hope by the power of the Holy Spirit" (Romans 15:13).

Moving in Hope

During life's difficult times, and even your most painful seasons, know these two things:

- As long as the Shepherd is in the dark valley with you, you are not without hope. Even if the darkness conceals the green pastures from your sight, your Shepherd will lead you to lie down in their midst.
- Jesus' love for you is unfailing. No matter how strong or weak you feel, His love never wavers. Do you seem to be in a godforsaken place of loss, despair, or disease? Your Shepherd is with you. Even if you didn't see the bus coming, He did, and He has prepared the way for you.

Praying in Hope

Father, although I am struggling with the idea, I thank You that You truly are the God of all hope. May Your Spirit help me look to Jesus, who is the forever horizon of my hope and the author and perfecter of my faith. Amid the darkness, let Your good Spirit reveal the horizon at the edge of my current valley of shadows. As I lean on Your indwelling Spirit to strengthen my will and urge me forward, may Jesus, my light, pull me into the future that lies beyond the shadows and lead me one step at a time. In His name I pray. Amen.

DAY
2

Pay Attention

> When you turn to the right or when you turn to the left, your ears shall hear a word behind you, saying, "This is the way; walk in it."
>
> Isaiah 30:21

Thoughts of Hope

Even in our fast-paced world, the truth continually beckons. Signs are flashing around you and within you. The better tuned your attention is, the sooner you will see them. Like my dream before my dark season, the signs are telling you where you are spiritually, physically, emotionally, and psychologically. Although they are there for your benefit, they seem to show up at the most inconvenient times, amid the pressures of the moment.

Beloved, pressure is always present. There is no convenient time to pay attention. The least convenient time is when the bus is coming at you and it's too late to step out of the way. So listen to your body's warning signs before the bus approaches. Value yourself enough to act on what they are telling you. Care for yourself the way you care for those you love. Observe what your mind and body are saying, or you will be forever driven by the things you think you need or ought to do. Pay attention to your feelings and honor them. Yes, they can be fickle. And yes, you are called to live by faith rather than by sight. But faith does not ignore feelings. Faith considers feelings in the light of truth.

You have probably heard teachings about how your feelings undermine your faith. I've heard those teachings, too. They sound good because they encourage us to "be strong in faith" and "overcome." We were built to overcome, but our feelings are not our enemy. Such an idea misunderstands how we were created to function, and many Christians have sacrificed their well-being because of it.

There's no condemnation here. I ignored my feelings for years, "blowing and going," as they say, and burning the candle at both ends. I exercised every single day and still do. I took loads of vitamins and ate the right foods (and still do). I was pretty proud to say that I took no prescribed medications. But I wasn't paying attention to what I was feeling. I ignored my stress levels and the effects of my sleep deprivation and restlessness. I shushed the voice that warned me to slow down, and I willed my way through my exhaustion. Finally, my body refused my demands, and I landed in the darkest place I ever could have imagined.

Does my experience resonate with you? Are you trying too hard to perform? Are you doing it at an unsustainable level? If you feel compelled to accomplish everything that is demanded of you and everything you demand of yourself, the answer to all three questions is yes. You are running on adrenaline more than you realize and becoming your own worst enemy—not because you want to crash and burn but because you have taken on more than you were called to carry.

Running on adrenaline can become a way of life, but it won't work forever. It *is* the perfect way to lose touch with what your body and mind are saying. You might be performing like a superhero and getting high marks from those who marvel at your strength, but you might also be running on fumes. Adrenaline will conceal your exhaustion, maybe even for decades, but eventually, something will have to give. And that something will force you to pay attention.

To honor your feelings does not dishonor God. You are fearfully and wonderfully made with the divinely ordained ability to have feelings. If you heed them, they will tell you what you need to know to overcome for the long term. So slow down. Take your foot off the accelerator long enough to get the rest you need. Give yourself permission to stay healthy in mind and body. Establish better sleep patterns. Observe the Sabbath and regularly disconnect from your daily routine.

If you are suffering from anxiety, pay attention and get whatever help you need. Let your pain expose the drivers that are contributing to your suffering. God already knows about your anxiety. So go ahead! Lay it (and any other issue) bare before Him. Allow Him to expand your hope by showing you better ways forward. He will lead you to healthier, happier days, in Him, with Him, and by His Holy Spirit.

Moving in Hope

If you learn anything from life's dark seasons, learn to pay attention. Your feelings are there for a reason. Consider this:

- Your feelings are important. What makes them feelings is the fact that you feel them in your body.
- When your body tells you how stressed, angry, or burned out you are, listen. Ignoring these signs means ignoring a trustworthy witness, the voice of the very Spirit who calls you toward life.
- Remember that faith does not call you to ignore the truth. It gives you the courage to face your feelings and learn from them.

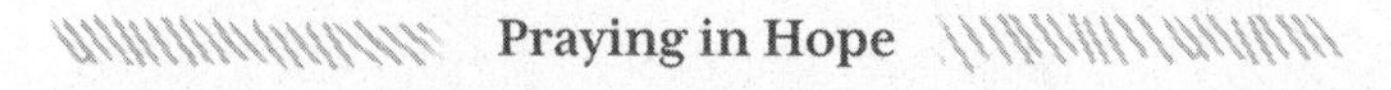

Praying in Hope

Father, my anxiety has gotten the best of me, and I am finding it hard to rest and let go. Forgive my penchant for controlling what is beyond my control and wanting to know what is beyond my knowing. Please help me not to ignore the truth but to pay attention as my body tells me to slow down. Help me not only to discern my body's cries but to heed them. Thank You for letting me feel the pain of my anxiety in my body. May it teach me to trust You and not myself. In Jesus' name, amen.

Honor Your Humanness

As a father has compassion for his children, so the LORD has compassion for those who fear him. For he knows how we were made; he remembers that we are dust.

Psalm 103:13–14

Thoughts of Hope

Has today gotten off to a rough start? Did yesterday turn out like a blooper reel? What can I say but, "Welcome to humanity!" As blessed as you are in Christ, you can still have "one of those days." Just saying something the wrong way can cause a commotion you never saw coming. And what if you lose your cool at work, forget a loved one's birthday, or miss what you thought was your golden opportunity? Add any physical or emotional pain to the mix, and you might wonder who you are and what you are doing wrong.

You are human. And if you haven't blundered or suffered yet, there's still time. You are wonderfully made, but perfection is not part of your makeup. If perfection is your goal, disappointment will be your reward. Perfectionism is like an octopus; its tentacles can strangle you emotionally. I know because I lived with that beast for years and believed what it told me: that I was not good enough, smart enough, or talented enough.

Your ups and downs, foibles, and mistakes—yes, even your failures—are signs that you are human, a fact of which God is well aware. Whatever today brings, His love will not fail you. He loves you when you excel, and He loves you when you fall short. After all, He created you to be human. So honor your humanness! His perfect love does not demand perfection from you. Instead, His love develops your humanness into something more beautiful each day. He is with you through your mistakes and your pain, and He is inching you ever closer to being the fully human person He created you to be.

That is God's desire. He did not create you as an angelic being. If He wanted to make you an angel, He would have done exactly that. But He had other plans. He created angels to be angels, and He created you to be you—an embodied spirit for whom being spiritual means being human. When you falter, remember that your humanity is not a defect. It is God's precise intent, and none of your human frailties can nullify it. He chose to make you a human being in His own image and likeness (see Genesis 1:26). That is His Word.

God did not stop there. His incarnate Son came to show all of us what being human is all about. He never modeled the angelic because that was not His mission. The Nicene Creed says He "was made human." The fully divine Son had to also be fully human to complete His salvific work. Would He have done that if being human was evil? No! The fully human, fully divine Son of God took on flesh and showed us how to love and die well, the way He did. Even now, our Redeemer's love is working in us, bringing our humanness closer and closer to the divine intent. Until we receive our resurrected bodies, His work continues.

Beloved, God knows what He is doing. In His love, He covers us. Yet He is not a God of cover-ups. So often, we dishonor our humanity by trying to conceal it. Like Adam and Eve trying to cover their nakedness, we disguise our weaknesses and sin, virtually burying ourselves in the process. Why are we so afraid to be ourselves? The Scriptures say that we are sinners (see Romans 7:14–20). Our fragmentation is an inescapable fact of this life. Jesus knows that but never rejects us. Instead, He puts us together again, re-membering us by His Spirit. Even in our brokenness, we become acceptable before God because of what the Son did.

In Christ, *you* became acceptable. So welcome to humanity! Put your journey to becoming fully human in His trustworthy hands.

Moving in Hope

If you feel distressed by a situation you mishandled or by negative thoughts, emotions, and feelings, you have a lot of company. Every person who has lived long enough to falter knows how you feel. This sin-stained world affects us all. Simply lean into the Savior. Acknowledge what you are feeling and bring every situation to Him. Allow Him to pick up your fragments and re-member you. Then honor your humanness. He does!

Praying in Hope

Father, thank You that Your love never fails, even when I feel like failing is what I do best. My brokenness is affecting how I see myself and the world around me. Help me to see past my pain and embrace Jesus as my healer. Open my eyes to His touch as He mends my wounds. Help me to accept my humanness and receive Your love, Your mercy, Your forgiveness, and Your grace. Remind me that apart from Jesus, I will always be far from adequate, yet in Him, every good thing becomes possible. In His name I pray. Amen.

Stop Digging

> Discipline always seems painful rather than pleasant at the time, but later it yields the peaceful fruit of righteousness to those who have been trained by it.
>
> Hebrews 12:11

Thoughts of Hope

Have you ever thought you were dealing with reality only to discover that what you embraced was a lie? Don't be shocked; the Scriptures warn that your own heart can trick you. Mine fooled me, and I fell for it—hard.

Jeremiah said that "the heart is more deceitful than all else" (Jeremiah 17:9 NASB). I know that verse backward and forward and probably preached it both ways. Yet I missed its application when there were signs of trouble ahead. Instead of being disciplined in addressing the warnings, I ignored them—for years. Somehow, I failed or refused to realize that unless I changed my ways, I would pay the price. It was just a matter of time.

I did pay, and dearly. Looking back, I did what people do every day: I tried to bury my reality, believing I could deal with it at a more convenient time. Of course, there was no such time. I simply created a bubble of magical thinking that allowed me to feel secure, even as I unraveled any semblance of security with my own hands. In retrospect, I conveniently replaced what was real with what I wanted to believe was real. After all, I was busy serving God and helping people. Those were and are my passions. I had reached the point in life where opportunities to serve came from every direction. So my heart convinced me that handling all of that was more important than noticing the danger ahead. I lived in blissful ignorance, as though endless seasons of stress and exhaustion would have no consequences.

You probably know how this burying thing works. To cope with the signs of trouble, we first erect façades that say everything is fine when it isn't. We continue to deceive ourselves through myriad forms of avoidance. Sometimes, we use "faith talk" to whitewash unpleasant realities. We carelessly say, "God is in control," or "I'm just waiting on the Lord." Or we procrastinate, believing that postponement will get us off the hook until the issue resolves itself. But issues rarely resolve themselves. And avoidance is not faith.

Faith confronts the issues, knowing they are no match for God's grace and mercy.

Have you been avoiding something you need to face? Did you try burying it, hoping it would disappear? Did your strategy only make matters worse? Then stop digging. What you bury alive stays alive and eventually resurfaces, stronger and with deeper roots than ever. Nothing disappears; it only festers in your unconscious mind and reappears in the form of anxiety, depression, and other forms of suffering. The tiny twinges you felt in the past can become intense suffering in the future. You may have postponed facing the matter until "tomorrow," but tomorrow eventually comes. The sooner you face the matter, the better off you will be.

Beloved, has tomorrow already arrived? Are you now immersed in what you tried to avoid? Has an old piece of unfinished business burrowed back into your conscious awareness and disrupted the whole of your life? How overwhelming that can be! It's like a tsunami of emotions that refuses to be constrained. Perhaps it has come because your mind and body decided that enough is enough. It's okay; let it be the start of your healing!

In such moments, the discipline of revisiting your unfinished business might seem too painful to bear. But you don't have to bear it in your own strength. You do it in the might of the One who gave you life. He saw this day coming, and He has prepared you for it. Let Him see you through, moment by moment, and "the peaceful fruit of righteousness" will surely follow.

Moving in Hope

You can stop digging by admitting that not everything is fine all the time. Even if you follow Christ faithfully, you live in a fallen world. When the pressure is on, you can be tempted to run from reality, bury an issue, and try to deal with it later. If you feel tempted in that way, pause. Then ask some questions.

- Ask yourself whether you can be okay even when not everything seems to be "fine."
- Ask the Lord to help you perceive what is "fine" in your life and what is façade.

Praying in Hope

Father, I have become more aware of the coping skills I learned from a very early age. I now realize that when life gets tough, I use these skills to avoid reality. By Your good Spirit, I also perceive that my avoidance strategies are not helping me. I confess that I have been afraid to face what isn't perfectly okay. Lord, forgive my fear. I have worked hard to avoid whatever seems less than good. But I don't want to neglect this inner issue any longer. Deliver me from the hurtful coping habits that have become so deeply embedded in my life. In Jesus' name, amen.

DAY

5

Facing the Unthinkable

Truly the thing that I fear comes upon me, and what I dread befalls me. I am not at ease, nor am I quiet; I have no rest, but trouble comes.

Job 3:25–26

Thoughts of Hope

Are your heart and mind at rest today? Is peace your portion? Or have rest and peace seemed to exit the scene? So many people—yes, even God's people—are experiencing anxiety. For some it is so severe as to be all-consuming. For others, it is a new experience that seemed to come out of nowhere. Either way, its waves of panic can be debilitating and disorienting and can leave you feeling uneasy in the familiar spaces that once brought you comfort.

Beloved, if you are experiencing that kind of pain, take heart. This season will pass, and you are not alone. In a tumultuous world, saying that we are on edge and unsure of what is next is an understatement. Absent the Holy Spirit's leading, we can barely know which way is up.

Anxiety and disorientation are exhausting, like nothing else I have experienced. Years ago, the only level-10 pain I could describe came from a kidney stone. That pain cut like a knife and hijacked my focus. Even with medication, the agony would not quit, and until I had surgery, the stone would not budge. But when the procedure was over, both the stone and the pain were gone.

Emotional anguish is not so easy to remove. If my anxiety could have been cut away the way my kidney stone was, I would have gone under the knife in a heartbeat. But it doesn't work that way. Dealing with my anxiety required me to do the unthinkable: I had to face the pain and not run from it. But who wants to run toward such suffering? No one! Instinct says to turn the other way and run as far and as fast as possible, as though fleeing an inferno.

Fleeing does not help. If you have tried it, you already know that wherever you go, your anxiety goes with you. And the harder you try to run from it, the more power you give it. The powers of darkness know that. So they use the unthinkable waves of anxiety to twist God's promises, telling you that you will be in your dark wood forever. The accuser will tell you that you "opened a door" and brought all manner of terror upon yourself. It's a clever trick, because when you are in your own dark wood, standing before a weathered (metaphorical) gravestone, you just might believe that you are under judgment in some area of your life.

The enemy's accusations are designed to amplify your trauma, so that what seems unthinkable claims to herald your destruction. It is a ruse! Whatever you do, *do not* surrender your praise or self-isolate. Lift your praises to God and allow someone in the faith whom you trust to remind you who you are. Their encouragement can help you stand and resist every satanic accusation.

That is what my dearest friend, Vinnie, did for me. I don't know what I would have done without him. He walked me through my dark wood and knew just how to reach me. He helped me to process my thoughts rather than run from them, always reminding me that God's everlasting arms were beneath me, lifting me above the waves (see Deuteronomy 33:27 NIV).

Do you feel like a torrent was sent from hell to finish you off? Let me say what Vinnie would have said: You are not forsaken. Evil will not swallow you whole. God has not overlooked your prayers for relief. Even when healing is not instantaneous and the Scriptures you recite don't zap the demons that seem to have descended upon you, God is upholding you. So lay every unthinkable part of your dark wood before God. You will find that it has less power than you thought. Go ahead and look it dead in the eye, because underneath you are the everlasting arms.

Moving in Hope

The wholeness that you need and want does not come from magical thinking or clever formulas. It comes from knowing the truth, experientially and deeply. As unwelcome as your suffering is, ask the Lord to help you embrace the learning opportunity it presents.

Allow God to test everything you think you believe. Be open to His touch as He strips away any misguided views that would keep you from wholeness. Pay attention as He puts His finger on anything that is inconsistent with His design for you. Nothing He removes is worth keeping, and nothing He gives you will do you anything but good. If you have any misconceptions about Scripture or about God, allow Him to shatter them and set you free!

Praying in Hope

Father, I believe You are teaching me to learn from my pain. Over the years, I have done a thorough job of teaching myself to run from my pain and avoid what seems unthinkable to me. But in this season, my error has caught up with me. What seems unthinkable is also real and worthy of my attention. Grant me by Your indwelling Spirit the inner strength to stand and face the pain head on. Teach me how to listen to it and learn from it, so that I can be freed from it. In Jesus' name, amen.

DAY

6

Put Awful in Its Place

Finally, brothers and sisters, whatever is true, whatever is honorable, whatever is just, whatever is pure, whatever is pleasing, whatever is commendable, if there is any excellence and if there is anything worthy of praise, think about these things.

Philippians 4:8

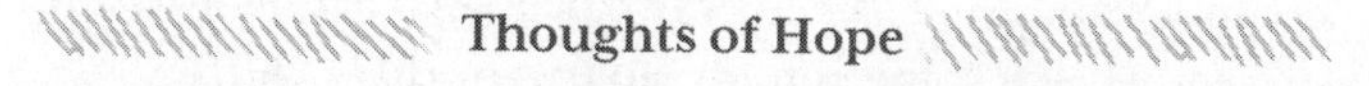

Thoughts of Hope

Do you lose perspective when you experience disappointment or pain? Does your current adversity taint even your memories? The answer is almost assuredly yes. Everyone processes their pain differently, but everyone eventually dwells on the past through the darkened lens of today's pain. This tendency forms a feedback loop that confirms the awfulness of the present situation and slathers it everywhere your mind goes. That is the nature of "awfulizing"—it effectively fixes your mind on how terrible you feel and increases your suffering.

I confess! I lived that script from beginning to end and back again. Of course, if you want to understand your anxious states and other forms of psychological pain, you have to look back and consider where you've been. But doing it endlessly from every conceivable angle (like I did) can take you someplace you do not want to go. Instead of discovering how and why you reached your dark wood, you can become so fixated on your reconstructed past pains that you project them even onto your future.

The mind works in curious ways, so that your memories are not the objective snapshots you might expect them to be. Instead, they are reconstructions that you piece together according to how you interpret past events. That means your impressions are naturally subjective. Your way of viewing and understanding the world is different from mine. How the world seems to you is not exactly how it seems to me. That's what makes eyewitness accounts of crimes and other events so confusing. Whether two people or five hundred are present when a scene unfolds, no two of them will describe it exactly the same way.

You filter what you observe and remember through the life you have lived so far. All of us acknowledge our individuality, yet we can often assume that our ruminations are objective and not quite individual. Both conditions cannot be entirely true at the same time, however. When you remember, you *re-member* or reconstruct the pieces of a past that no longer exists. You reassemble those pieces the best you can, but always in the context of a much bigger picture that shapes *how* you see things. Understanding this subjectivity is vital to your mental health.

Your remembering will never be 100 percent reliable. But go easy on yourself! It's not as though you willfully lie or fabricate fairy tales. You simply try to make sense of indelible impressions that were made on your psyche in a moment of time—and possibly in a chaotic and traumatic moment. Because those impressions are always incomplete, you try to make sense of them by filling in any gaps. You do this with ideas that come from the memories themselves.

Do you see how easily you can select memories to awfulize and confirm your pain? You could say it is a default setting that keeps you ruminating and plunging ever deeper into your dark wood. That is what my ruminating did and sometimes still tries to do. The longer and harder I ruminated, the more awful my despair became and the longer my healing was delayed.

Beloved, if you are experiencing that kind of torment, you can choose not to cooperate with it. When you catch yourself awfulizing, remind yourself (and the powers of darkness) that although your memories are not 100 percent trustworthy, God is entirely trustworthy. Let the One who was with you in your past help you to arrest endless ruminations in your present. Let His healing touch clarify your way of seeing so you can lay your past hurts to rest and project His goodness into your future.

Moving in Hope

Making sense of your past can aid healing, but overanalyzing it can increase your pain. Ruminating can become an almost unconscious practice because you don't always realize (1) when you are projecting your past and present experiences, and (2) when you are accepting as "gospel" memories that are by nature incomplete.

Two things to remember about rumination:

- It can become an avoidance strategy that keeps you from dealing with your current reality by dwelling on the pain of your past.
- Each "rehearsal" can trigger new fears and convince you that your current, temporary pain is a permanent condition.

Praying in Hope

Father, my demotivating re-membering has worn me out. I have acted more often on the false fragments of my memories than on Your promise of my future. This has blinded me in the present moment to Your ever-abiding presence and love. With Your help, I will do my best to let go of my endless ruminating, and I will more consciously resist projecting reconstructed memories into my present moment and my future. As I try to make sense of what happened in the past, I will place my eyes on Jesus, who remembers and understands perfectly. In His name I pray. Amen.

DAY
7

Being *Here*

Where can I go from your spirit? Or where can I flee from your presence? If I ascend to heaven, you are there; if I make my bed in Sheol, you are there. If I take the wings of the morning and settle at the farthest limits of the sea, even there your hand shall lead me, and your right hand shall hold me fast.

Psalm 139:7–10

Thoughts of Hope

No one is exempt from suffering. If that thought enters your heart like a dark cloud, let me point out the silver lining: Suffering releases your growth potential. You develop beyond your current state largely through the things you endure. Pain initiates your search for answers, and those answers help you to become more ruthlessly honest about yourself, what you believe, and how you relate to God and people. Pain also serves to locate you. If you pay attention, it will help you to know exactly where you are.

Therein lies the rub. When you're suffering, the last place you want to be is where you are. What you really want is *out*—out of your pain, out of a bad situation, even out of your own skin. Almost any place on the planet seems like a better one than *here*. Ask me how I know. The first minutes of my severe anxiety seemed utterly unbearable. When it lingered for years, I thought jumping out of my own skin (if only I could!) would be my only hope of relief.

"Getting out of one's skin" is a metaphorical idea that points to what we all desire—to transcend our current limitations and ascend into heaven. In Psalm 139:8, David alludes to this when he talks about making his bed in hell. If you feel as though you have already made your bed in hell, you might lose sight of the rest of David's point—that God's Spirit is in your "hell" with you. David understood that his own yearning for transcendence was satisfied in the presence of the living God from whom he could not be separated. Being in that presence was David's sanctified way of jumping out of his own skin! So he worshiped in his *here* and essentially said, "Even if I do make my bed in Sheol, You are there."

No matter where your *here* is or how you got there, God's Spirit is present to lift you above it. No one is perfect before

God. All of us have messed up. Some of our mistakes have added to our suffering, but not all of our troubles result from wrongs we committed. Regardless of any part we played, our trouble is not beyond God's mercy. As Paul explains in Romans 7, we were born into the inner conflict between wanting to do good and knowing that sin dwells in us. The apostle captures our predicament in his cry: "Wretched person that I am!" (Romans 7:24).

Is that your cry? Then let Paul's transparency comfort you. When you feel as though suffering is the locus of your life, Paul's approach to the struggle will shed light. He wanted what you and I want—to be delivered from every wretched state. It doesn't matter what his issue was or what yours is. Eating from the Tree of the Knowledge of Good and Evil is the root of all human suffering, and each of us has eaten there.

What matters is that you long to be delivered, and your Deliverer is present! That is why Paul's testimony is so life-giving; he understood how his deliverance would come. He didn't seek a technique of "five easy steps" or "seven ways to freedom." He didn't ask, "What will deliver me?" He asked, "*Who* will deliver me?" (Romans 7:24 ESV, emphasis added). What he wanted more than deliverance was the Deliverer Himself, the perfect lover of his soul.

The hardest thing about being *here*, in the place of your pain, is the thought that you might be there alone. I can assure you that you aren't. Wherever *here* is, He is. Your deliverance is with Him, and your deliverance is in Him (see Ephesians 1:7–17).

Moving in Hope

When misery finds you, what you believe about your pain can make all the difference. Do you believe you "got yourself into this mess" and must get yourself out of it? Most of us have been taught some version of that idea. But we are not our own deliverers, and the mercy of God would not be mercy at all unless it applied to the messes we make.

Maybe, like David, you wonder whether you have made your bed in hell. That's a good question, but here's a better one: "Who is here with me?" The one true God can be with you in places no person can go. So take your rest, beloved; He is even with you in your own skin.

Praying in Hope

Father, when I forget, please remind me that my pain is part of being human, and I am never alone in my struggles. Lord Jesus, show me again how my suffering leads to learning and growth. Thank You for enduring all You did so You could come to me in my pain and show me the way through and out. You know me better than I know myself, and You know the way. I trust You and love You. Restore my confidence in Your abiding presence and love. Move me forward by Your Spirit within me. Amen.

DAY

8

Being with Your Pain

> You have kept count of my tossings; put my tears in your bottle. Are they not in your record? Then my enemies will retreat in the day when I call. This I know, that God is for me. In God, whose word I praise, in the Lord, whose word I praise.
>
> Psalm 56:8–10

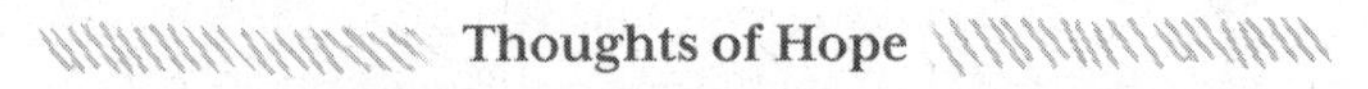

Thoughts of Hope

When you come right down to it, our desire to be delivered is our yearning to separate from the unwelcome companion known as *pain*. Do you remember what I shared about magical thinking? It is a kind of bubble in which we separate what is uncomfortably real from what we wish were real. It is an unconscious strategy, a way of running from the realities we'd rather ignore. So when circumstances overwhelm us, we console ourselves by wishing them away. Our avoidance seems to work at first, but it never works for long.

When intense anxiety gripped every cell in my being and every thought that crossed my mind, I thought my pain was a problem to be avoided like the plague. So I tried desperately to separate myself from it. The harder I tried, the worse it got. When a professional told me that I needed to *be with my pain*, I thought he was kidding me. I was expecting him to show me the quickest way out of my agony!

In my torment, the "prescription" for being with my pain made no sense. Yet when I "took my medicine" and stopped running, the pain began to subside. That is partly because of how fear works. The drive to separate yourself from pain springs from the fear of pain, which is instinctual. You don't naturally run toward things that will hurt you. But being *with* your pain doesn't mean you're chasing it down or begging for more. If the pain is there, it's there. Refusing to acknowledge it won't change that. It will, however, create an internal dissonance that produces more pain, emotionally and psychologically.

Is facing your pain easy? Not at first. You and I are not geared that way. Culturally, as Christians, we believe that if Jesus died to set us free, we should never have to go through hell. The idea sounds sensible, except that in the bigger, eternal picture, God will use your suffering to enlarge you. You are not called to give yourself over to any form of death. Not at all. Death is your enemy, and you resist it. But I can promise you that God will never squander your pain. David said to God, "You have . . . put my tears in your bottle. Are they not in your record?" Imagine! Your tears are so precious to God that He collects and keeps them!

Do you struggle with the paradigm of growth through pain? I have been there! In an individualistic, have-it-your-way culture, the idea seems nonsensical. But the saint and mystic Teresa of Avila grasped the divine sense of her suffering and beautifully described it, writing, "I realize better every day what grace our Lord has shown me in enabling me to understand the blessings of suffering so that I can peacefully endure the want of happiness in earthly things since they pass so quickly."[1]

Out of your suffering will come mysterious blessings! As the Lord catches today's tears in His bottle, aspects of His grace become visible in the thick of your dark wood. You are not called to prostrate yourself for the sake of misery. Nor are you called to suffer in Christ's place. But in all your affliction, you can prostrate yourself before the One who made you and understands all things. Take your distress to Him, and He will take you through!

Moving in Hope

Beloved, if you are suffering today, allow yourself to (1) be with your pain and (2) be drawn by His Spirit into worship. He is with you in your darkest valley, holding and keeping you. He is not punishing you or sending harassment your way. Even if you never gain the full understanding of what you are enduring in this season, you can be certain that He understands it and has heard your every cry. Your tears will not be shed in vain. The One who loves you the most is making a way where there seems to be no way at all.

Praying in Hope

Father, I come before You, relying on Your abiding presence and the power of Your indwelling Spirit to help me cope in my anguish. My suffering is real. Sometimes, I feel like the pain is big, and I am small. I admit that the trouble can seem more powerful than both me and You. Lord Jesus, remind me that nothing I face will ever be more than You and I can handle. Lead me in a plain path because of the enemies of my soul. Thank You for Your great grace and mercy in the midst of this challenge. I pray this in Your holy name. Amen.

DAY
9

Perplexity All Around

> We are afflicted in every way but not crushed, perplexed but not driven to despair, persecuted but not forsaken, struck down but not destroyed, always carrying around in the body the death of Jesus, so that the life of Jesus may also be made visible in our bodies.
>
> 2 Corinthians 4:8–10

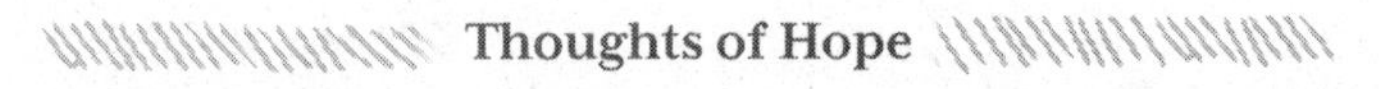

Thoughts of Hope

Life is complicated. Perplexity is increasing and can bear down when you feel least able to handle it. With uncertainty so prevalent at the societal level, you cannot help but feel it in your corner of this life. Things are shifting, *and fast*. The rules you grew up with—even those that have been around for millennia—are morphing before your eyes. To imagine that you would not be affected by such dynamics is to believe that ignorance is bliss.

Are you painfully aware of perplexity or even up against what seems like an onslaught? Maybe you did your due diligence in a business or medical matter, conferred with trusted counselors, and prayed about how to proceed, only to experience what looks like a worst-case scenario. Up is down, black is white, and suddenly, you can do nothing right. Everyone who trusted you yesterday doubts you today. You feel like a failure, and there seems to be nothing left to say except, "If I had seen the bus coming, I would have stepped out of the way."

Is that where you are? In such moments, beloved, it can be hard to breathe. Maybe your mortgage is overdue, your children are making poor choices, and the person you love the most has let you down. It isn't always about the "big problems," however. Sometimes all the little things pile up, and you can't help but wonder whether you have missed God altogether. That kind of perplexity can claim space in your head until it commandeers your emotions, feelings, and body in ways you never saw coming.

So take heed. If you are becoming more apprehensive, don't brush it off. If your focus is becoming fragmented and more difficult to muster, take note. You may be reacting to unprecedented levels of anxiety. Such pressures exact a heavy toll. Even if you are in excellent shape and eating well, don't casually tell yourself, "I can handle this." Instead, be aware that such stressors can leave their mark, and you need to acknowledge them.

The powers of darkness know just how to exploit such moments. They will tell you that you are incapable, unworthy, or incompetent. The more readily you accept their accusations, the more quickly new accusations will come. I can testify to their ferocity and ability to overwhelm, so beware. Instead of accepting them and heaping judgment upon yourself, take a step back. Be gentle and gracious with yourself, just as you would be with a loved one who is under pressure. Instead of assuming that you are responsible for everything that is broken, remember that you are a human being. Take stock of what you are up against. Ask God to show you what is really going on. Let Him search your heart and reveal what is happening within so you can learn and grow from it. Be still long enough for Him to reveal what is really happening around you. Listen, and He will lay it bare.

I often urge our congregation to slow down to the speed of revelation. It takes time to process your experiences and hear God's voice amid the chaos. Give yourself the space to learn at your own pace. Recognize that when you are in pain, you need even more grace. You might learn more slowly when you are pressured or perplexed. But God is always patient with you; therefore, you can be patient with yourself. You are His, dear one, and you are worth it.

Moving in Hope

When perplexity is all around and you feel adrift in a strange, dark wood, you can become impatient with yourself and with God. Here's what I mean: If you do not give yourself the grace and emotional space to grow during a crisis time, you risk missing the very answer and healing you have longed to receive. It doesn't mean that God is not speaking; it just means you have not positioned yourself to hear His voice above the clatter all around you.

The unfortunate irony is that we tend to shut out God precisely when we need Him the most. We tread His grace and patience underfoot as we hurry ourselves along to fix whatever is broken, only to realize that we are not God. Slow down. Be patient with yourself and with God, and allow His answers to fill your heart.

Praying in Hope

Father, I feel boxed into a corner, where the enemy has put the squeeze on me. Remind me that You will enlarge me in my distress even as You enlarged David. Help me to remember that, even in the tightest place, You are abundantly available to help me and love me into life. As the powers of darkness attempt to exploit this sensitive season in my life, help me to take a breath, step back, and resist their accusations. I put my trust in You and You alone. Thank You, Lord Jesus, that by Your Spirit I will overcome this season of perplexity. Amen.

DAY
10

Beauty for Ashes

> The spirit of the LORD GOD is upon me because the LORD has anointed me; he has sent me to bring good news to the oppressed . . . to give them a garland instead of ashes, the oil of gladness instead of mourning, the mantle of praise instead of a faint spirit.
>
> Isaiah 61:1, 3

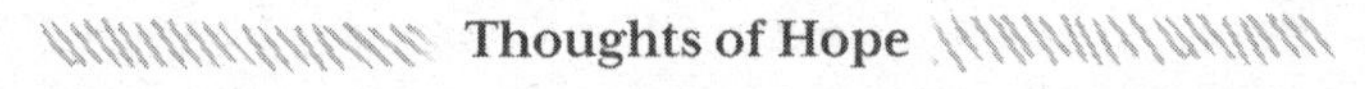

Thoughts of Hope

Have you entered your darkest season? Have you been transported to the seeming graveyard of your hopes? Are even your beliefs reduced to ashes? I understand that level of grief, and I dare not minimize it. But I bring these glad tidings:

Even your darkest wood is not entirely dark, and the embers of your hopes are still alive.

Beloved, your time of struggle is the cusp of your next season. You can cross it with the confidence that comes through transformation. Strange as it seems, certain changes only happen in your most troubled times. They are the ones that leave you shouting, "I once . . . was blind, but now I see."[1] You might think as I did, that your dark season threatens your very existence. Extreme suffering can trigger such thoughts, and for good reason. But you are not as far out on a limb as you think. Nor is refuge as distant as your pain would suggest.

What seems like an existential threat may be more an accusation from the powers of darkness than you realize. Don't misunderstand me. I'm not saying that your darkest season will leave no mark. You cannot navigate life's crossroads and be untouched by them. Struggles of great magnitude shake whatever can be shaken. Your beliefs and suppositions are tested, and that testing makes for unease. But the lover of your soul is not out to destroy you. Not everything that is shaken is of His Kingdom, and what is His will stand in the end.

When you exit your dark season, you will travel lighter. Your trial will have winnowed out beliefs that once distorted your point of view. As you press through your suffering and into God, He will adjust your ways of being and seeing. Like me, you can find yourself saying, "My suffering was terrifying, but I would not change it for anything. I now understand the crossroad that confronted me, and that understanding informs my life."

I will grant you that at the height of your suffering, the words you just read might barely graze your sense of overwhelm and fear. Linger over them anyway. Latch on to what you are hearing the best you can and don't let go. There was something beautiful about you before trouble came calling. But what seems poised to destroy you will leave behind a radiancy that was not possible before your dark season. You will discover a kind of strength you had not known before, a compassion for others that is never helpless but always engaged—an openness of heart that helps you to discern their traumas more acutely so you can love them more completely. You might become more open to certain ideas than you were in the past because God used your suffering to enlarge you. And having navigated your dark wood, you understand that no one is immune to hardship.

God is already giving you beauty for your ashes. You might be suffering and even fearful in this very moment, but please know that your experience is not occurring in a vacuum. You might feel as though you have been struck down and laid bare, but the Lord your God is covering you. As your pain unfolds in His presence, your heart is exposed to His marvelous healing touch. Your suffering is not in vain, and from it something very beautiful will come!

Moving in Hope

Pain can preoccupy your consciousness and usurp your waking thoughts. Ask the Lord to help you not be overrun by the weight of your suffering. With Him, you can withstand it and enjoy an unexpected "reward"—the powerful transformation that only follows your greatest ordeals. Let your trial bind you more consciously to the One who has never abandoned you—the Lamb who ever stands as freshly slain on the throne of the universe.

Praying in Hope

Father, I am aware that underneath me are Your everlasting arms—Your Son and Your Spirit. Had they not undergirded me, I could easily have fallen into the endless abyss of my pain. Remind me that somewhere at the bottom of all of this difficulty, a gift awaits my discovery and will open a door to a genuinely hopeful future. Lead me across the cusp into what is ahead. Give me eyes to see it in the dark. Fan the embers of my hope and help me to travel lighter, day by day. In Jesus' name, amen.

DAY

11

Not a Loser

For though the LORD is high; he regards the lowly, but the haughty he perceives from far away. Though I walk in the midst of trouble, you preserve me against the wrath of my enemies; you stretch out your hand, and your right hand delivers me.

Psalm 138:6–7

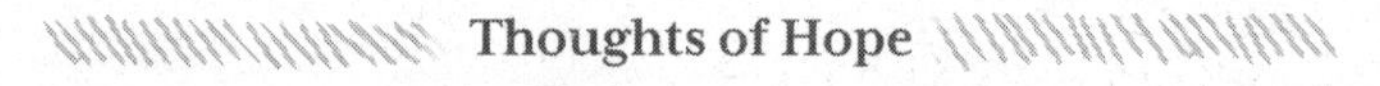

Thoughts of Hope

When you are in a season of trial, you know it. But it still might be hard to articulate your feelings or even identify them. Your season can have the strangeness of a dream state. Like the dream I shared in the introduction, it can take time to sort through all it means. That is not surprising, because your dark wood is by nature a disorienting place. It can leave you feeling like a stranger to yourself, or like a loser in a world full of winners.

That is what happens when a new level of chaos skews your perspective about the world, about what really matters, and about your own identity. Not all of the skewing is negative. Transitions are liminal spaces that stretch your capacity and will. They tug on the boundaries of your understanding, and for better or worse, they redraw them. The key is to distinguish what is true from what is deceptive.

Even when it hurts, there is no better medicine than the truth. Why? Because our thinking is not always as sound as we believe it to be. Then trouble comes and ruthlessly exposes every loose connection with the truth that we have tolerated. That's when life's liminal spaces heighten our awareness and confuse our senses all at once. You could say they are acid tests that burn through our façades and lay bare our underpinnings, including our misbeliefs, misunderstandings, and unhealthy coping mechanisms.

Are you experiencing that kind of test? Does anguish seem to be sifting you and your views? Are you shocked to find that something you believed failed the test? Don't despair. There is no escaping the reality of the culture around you. No matter how much you love Jesus, you have been tutored by prevailing mindsets, and some have permeated your way of seeing. Without your conscious awareness, issues, events, and experiences of human suffering have left their imprint on you. You might have certain beliefs about what it means to succeed or fail, be poor or rich, a winner or a loser. Those beliefs are more fluid than you think.

You take your beliefs with you into your dark night of the soul, and in that season's deep shadows, what you think and believe comes into stark relief. After all, the unexpected has shaken you to your core, and you are primed to react. You feel threatened and vulnerable and are prone to making emotional, fear-driven assessments of who you are. Those judgments don't come out of thin air. They draw on the beliefs and misunderstandings that have been untested until now.

So *are* you a loser in a world full of winners? Is that what your present difficulty is telling you? Or is the accuser using against you everything you thought you knew or believed? We live in a culture where everyone wants to win all the time. That is not exactly a Jesus idea. Instead, it makes people who have lost something feel like they don't belong.

The fact is that all of us lose things. It could be peace of mind, health, a home, a marriage, a limb, a dream, or even a child. Does Jesus run from "losers" and seek out the "winners" whose lives appear to be intact? Beloved, you know the answer. He gravitates to the suffering, the disenfranchised, and the disillusioned, distressed, and downcast. He searches for those who feel like sheep without a shepherd, and He walks with them through life's shadowy valleys. The Wonderful Counselor knows the soul's dark night firsthand. Whatever seems lost, or however lost you feel, He will not exclude you from His glorious presence. You are His, and in His love, you can only win.

Moving in Hope

Whether you feel like you lost something due to anxiety, depression, financial trouble, or a broken heart, Jesus knows you by name and loves you with an everlasting love. He is not somewhere "out there." If you are His, He is within you and will never leave you.

- In the midst of the battle, cling to Him! Take every accusatory thought that puts you on the outside looking in and subject it to His love. Such thoughts do not come from Jesus but from the accuser who opposes Him and all who are His.
- When you feel lost, disenfranchised, disillusioned, distressed, or downcast, let your Advocate handle your case. He never loses.

Praying in Hope

Father, I know Paul said he was not ignorant of the devil's wiles. Truth be told, I feel in this season as though I am ignorant of them. Yet Your Spirit is teaching me how the enemy often presents his accusations as questions that make me second-guess You and myself. By Your Spirit, please help me to recognize the accuser's veiled voice more quickly so that, when his lies seem poised to overwhelm me, I can effectively respond with the sword of the Spirit. I affirm it shall be well, because of Jesus. In His name I pray. Amen.

DAY
12

Not Resignation but Acceptance

So we do not lose heart. Even though our outer nature is wasting away, our inner nature is being renewed day by day. For our slight, momentary affliction is producing for us an eternal weight of glory beyond all measure.

2 Corinthians 4:16–17

Thoughts of Hope

It is possible that this morning delivered a rude awakening to your doorstep. Worry may have haunted every moment since. Bad news sometimes takes your breath away. It might seem that everything you have said or done over your lifetime has been for naught. In such moments, you might easily resign yourself to your troubles, but I pray you won't.

There is a way forward that involves neither resignation nor denial. It is simply to *accept* your struggle as it is and pour out your heart to your heavenly Father. You might not know what to do or where to begin. You might not understand what really happened. But you can acknowledge where you are and lay your ordeal before the only One who can see you all the way to the matter's end.

Acceptance might not look or sound like shouting ground, but it is a key to your well-being. Telling yourself the truth is therapeutic and can open unexpected ways forward. Accepting your situation is not a passive act, like resignation is. You are not surrendering to trouble; you are asserting your trust in God, knowing that He cannot be overwhelmed by *anything*. From that position, you can rest and lean forward.

Does acceptance still seem challenging? It did to me. I had conditioned myself to see it as a threat. I thought I could resist any constraining situation through sheer willpower. But my willpower had met its match. Severe anxiety had a will of its own—a strong will that refused to be broken. There was no "willing" or "rebuking" my way out of it. The harder I fought, the deeper I sank into defeat. (Operating in pride usually has that effect.)

Ignoring the situation served me no better. As depth psychologist Carl Jung said, "We cannot change anything until we accept it. Condemnation does not liberate, it oppresses."[1] I can attest to that oppression! It kept me entangled in a battle that wasn't mine. Believing that my suffering was demonic and therefore illegitimate, I fought it tooth and nail, convinced that God would not expect me to endure it. So I "cooperated" with Him by rebuking the whole situation. How wrong I was, and what a price I paid for my oversimplified theology! Nothing changed, except that my suffering worsened. It was a quandary that was hard to reconcile.

You may be in a similar bind. Something in your life may be causing great pain, and it seems to drain the very life from you. You may have tried all the methods you learned from books and teachings, only to realize that they are not working. The answers that once provided at least temporary relief are no longer of any use, and absolutely nothing is leading you toward your deliverance.

Beloved, why not take that as a clue that God is leading you toward unexpected truths? When you embrace them, they won't just answer your cries today; they will serve you throughout your lifetime. Remember: Your survival is not in your hands. You are in God's hands. From that blessed position, you can safely accept your current reality. You can trust that what seems like a life sentence is actually a season with an end point. And when you least expect it, your trial can hand you surprising treasures. *Accept them.*

Moving in Hope

Accepting a challenging season requires openness to a reality in God that you cannot yet see. If you place your faith in your willpower or ability to stand strong, you are demonstrating not your faith but a misplaced sense of pride. Denying your current reality can only increase the burden on your already taxed psyche. Instead of arming yourself to the teeth with theological shortcuts, why not heed what you're experiencing and accept where you are? Honor your emotions, however painful they might be. Then offer them up as worship and prayer to the God who keeps you.

Praying in Hope

Father, I am done running from my pain, suffering, fears, and anxieties. Today, I choose to stand in this truth: Your Son and Your Spirit are not only with me but in me, and they are guiding me to streams of living water. Lead me into unexpected truths that will sustain me throughout my days. I affirm that trouble won't last always. Help me to have a made-up mind, believing that I am going to get through this valley of shadows and to the other side with resources I never knew were mine. In Jesus' name, amen.

DAY

13

Check Your Thoughts

You desire truth in the inward being; therefore teach me wisdom in my secret heart. Purge me with hyssop, and I shall be clean; wash me, and I shall be whiter than snow. . . . Create in me a clean heart, O God, and put a new and right spirit within me.

Psalm 51:6–7, 10

Thoughts of Hope

Sometimes, you cannot see the forest for the trees. It doesn't matter how educated or well-intentioned you are. It doesn't even matter how ably you have helped other people through their trying seasons. When you are knee-deep in your own chaos, your ways of thinking can blind you to things that are in plain sight. Just when you most need God's help, you can miss or misunderstand even His answer to your most fervent prayer.

Of course, your thinking doesn't only get fuzzy on your worst days. Distortions are a fact of life and are present in good times and bad. They come from the filters and biases that develop as your life unfolds. But they are sneaky. Everyone has them, and everyone can see them in other people. But do you see your own blind spots? Probably not, because they are hidden in the recesses of your unconscious mind. From there, they have the freedom to muddle your outlook and make the obvious seem invisible.

According to experts, "cognitive distortion is a normal psychological process that can occur in all people to a greater or lesser extent."[1] In other words, your distortions don't separate you from the human race. Nor do they disqualify you from being delivered! The answer to this human condition is to prayerfully become more aware of how your own mind works. Check your thoughts. Pay attention to the reactions, judgments, and patterns that you find yourself repeating. Do you jump to conclusions or tend to cast blame? Do you feel the need to always be right or to label people on the basis of their imperfections? These cognitive distortions become ingrained and unconscious, and they blind you to what is really going on.

Instead of responding to life on autopilot, watch where your thinking goes. I found a pattern in my own life that contributed to my extended season of anxiety. From the outset of the ordeal, I was fiercely determined to fight my negative emotions, which I had classified as being demonic. Eventually, I recognized my mindset and its roots: I had taken Ephesians 6:12 as "proof" that my battle was demonic. Of course, Paul was right—we do not fight against flesh and blood. But not every contrary circumstance involves demons. I had overgeneralized the verse and applied it in a way that is common but incorrect. That caused me to misunderstand my anxiety and ignore its causes. You could say that demons did not hold me captive; my self-sabotaging thoughts did. My worst enemy was *me*!

When you become consciously aware of an unconscious stronghold, certain self-defeating habits lose their power. Uncovering even a seemingly small misunderstanding can expose the entire system of faulty thinking that it generates. Will the discovery end your suffering overnight? Maybe not. But the flawed thought process that once undermined you will disintegrate. Instead of fighting fake culprits, you can address the real issue and grow—spiritually, emotionally, and psychologically.

Beloved, there is no quick fix where growth is concerned. But when you open your heart to more truth, you reach new places of maturity in Christ. Through faith and patience, you can inherit the promises and stand firm, even on the hardest of days. So ask God to open your eyes to how you think, and give yourself the space to mature. When you check your thoughts, you move toward healing.

Moving in Hope

Clear thinking is an essential ingredient of freedom. What torments you today can be rooted in distortions you embraced in the past. They come in various ways. Some come through the culture, and some are propagated through your family system. Others come through faulty teachings or misrepresentations of Scripture. No matter where or how they originate, you can uncover them.

First, understand that all human beings are inclined toward distortions of thoughts. Second, seek divine guidance. Third, enlist the help of trusted friends or professionals who can provide the feedback that encourages objectivity. Be open to the provision of God; it can come in unexpected ways.

Praying in Hope

Father, by Your Spirit I realize more each day how easily my thinking and self-talk become distorted, and how readily I lose clarity. I deeply desire to change the way in which I see what is unfolding. Holy Spirit, help me to see it through Jesus' eyes. And Jesus, as I learn to see this way, teach me how to make meaning from what is happening—not as I once did, but differently. Help me to discern what is happening in relation to what You are working in my life. You are changing me from the inside out, and I thank You! In Your precious name, amen.

DAY

14

What If?

> You who sit down in the High God's presence, spend the night in Shaddai's shadow, say this: "GOD, you're my refuge. I trust in you and I'm safe!"
>
> Psalm 91:1–2 MSG

Thoughts of Hope

Life is never 100 percent certain. There are always variables and unknowns that are outside of your control. These uncertainties can lead to distress and the what-if thinking that affects your ability to cope. Sometimes, your what-ifs seem imminent, as though a merciless and ferocious beast were poised to pounce. Your boss tells you that he plans to retire and has sold his company. You have worked for him for twenty-five years. During that time, your position evolved into a unique expression of your skill sets. You wonder, *If that position disappears, then what? I'm not as young as I used to be, and this is the only job I've ever done. Will I find another position right away? What if I don't find something comparable? What if . . . ?*

Often there is no actual "beast" but only the lingering sense that something is bound to go wrong. An invisible monster stalks your every waking moment and keeps you from sleep for reasons you don't consciously understand. But whether your fears are concrete or elusive, they can trigger tirades of what-ifs. Unless you learn to corral them, they will haunt you night and day.

As a sentient being, you always experience a certain level of what-if thinking. Most of it is wasted on events that never materialize. Still, the cycle can be unrelenting—your what-ifs make you anxious, your anxiety feeds your what-ifs, and your what-ifs feed right back into your anxiety. This is especially true in seasons of severe turmoil when your peace seems nonexistent. Then your what-ifs loom even larger and flood your already inundated mind.

Putting your what-ifs to rest means first understanding their workings. Except in unusual cases of existential danger, they are tied to your overall outlook and the intangibles that involve your expectations, perspectives, and imaginations concerning the future. You can worry about losing your job even when you are in your twenties and your company is not up for sale. What-ifs might be assailing you right now, based not on any tangible present fears but on traumatic past experiences. These traumas don't always involve violent, catastrophic events. A job loss or a falling out with a loved one can leave a mark on your psyche. Some traumas, such as abuse and life-altering accidents, are typically more profound and can leave deep emotional and psychological wounds.

Beloved, has some type of trauma left its imprint on your life? Are you experiencing intrusive thoughts or memories? Do you find yourself in a heightened state of alert for no apparent reason? If so, what-if thinking can become a coping mechanism you unconsciously use to deal with your trauma. I used it. But instead of finding relief, I found myself in survival mode—a physiological fight-or-flight response to the what-ifs that I perceived as threats to my well-being.

Fight-or-flight is your body's way of meeting imminent danger. It is an appropriate response to a physical attack, building collapse, or other situation in which you must fight or run for your life. But when it responds to anxieties that are based on past events that no longer threaten you, the response itself is injurious.

What-ifs will present themselves, but they are not your master. Disengaging from patterned, persistent what-if thinking is a matter of increasing your self-awareness. A trusted friend can help you to adjust your perspective and know yourself better. A qualified therapist can help you identify any traumas and suggest healthier ways of resolving your fears. There is no shame in asking for help. You were not created to navigate this life alone. Above all, look to God. He knows you better than anyone does. Trust in Him, as the psalmist explained, and you are safe.

Moving in Hope

Your anxiety and what-if thinking are human experiences related to the existential anxiety that all people experience at some level. It involves your most primal fears, including "thoughts of death, the meaningless[ness] of life, or the insignificance of self." Existential thoughts are human thoughts about your meaning, purpose, and mortality.[1]

The intangibles that shape your anxiety—your expectations, perspectives, and imaginations about the future—are part of your life and consciousness. Become more consciously aware of them, and you will be less vulnerable to the anxiety they produce in the shadows of your unconscious mind.

Praying in Hope

Father, I have become so aware of my what-if thinking! It dawns on me that my awareness is not my doing. I see the issue because Your Spirit has put His finger on it. For that, I am forever grateful. You are showing me how deeply embedded this habit has become, and You are doing it so You can lead me out. My God, You are delivering me from this painful pattern by allowing me to experience this season. Thank You for inviting me to face it squarely and learn from it. Lead me on, Lord Jesus, I pray! Amen.

DAY
15

A Healing Life

Commit to Yahweh your way; trust also on him and he will act. Then he will bring forth your righteousness like the light, and your justice like the noonday.

Psalm 37:5–6 LEB

Thoughts of Hope

Did you learn some things growing up that you wish you could forget? For most people, their growing-up years were a mixed bag. Blended in with their good memories are some not-so-good ones and some lessons they don't realize they learned. In this fallen world, no one is raised apart from some dysfunction in the family system. We all have some bitter fruits in our family trees.

I joke that as an Italian American raised in New York City, I saw dysfunction as the norm. There is truth in the joke. I can see brokenness in my family line. You probably see brokenness in yours. And like me, you have lived with it. You might even be wondering why it persisted after you stood in a healing line where curses were supposed to be removed.

I believe in healing services because I believe in healing, but I also believe in telling the whole truth so that people can be made whole. Generational patterns represent decades or more of dysfunction that are rarely healed during a moment in time. I have been a pastor long enough to see generational patterns persist in families. I have pastored the children and their parents and grandparents. I have seen examples of transformation but also examples of persistent traits. Can healing come? Absolutely! But anything that is left broken in a family tree will only be passed down to the next generation.

Beloved, real healing occurs from the inside out. The same is true for the healing of families. I'm talking about the kind of healing that is not an event, but a lifelong process called sanctification. It simply means being conformed day by day to the image and likeness of Christ. It happens as we follow Him and allow the Holy Spirit to help us become fully human. The journey to wholeness affects every issue, fear, failure, and desire. Whatever pain you inherited and now carry is healed as you cleave to Christ, rest in His presence, and allow Him to be more fully revealed in you. That is how you glorify Him and leave a legacy for the generation that follows you. The process through which you are healed is the same process through which your generations are healed. But it is a process.

Does the idea of a process seem disappointing? I understand. We humans are not fond of solutions that take time. When I was in the thick of my dark wood, my therapist told me there was no quick fix for my pain. Was I disappointed? Sure! In fact, I wanted to give him a piece of my mind. But he was right. My restoration would come from the inside out as I acknowledged my brokenness, accepted where I was, and found new ways of approaching life's difficulties. My therapist was not a preacher, but he understood the healing process and saved me years of unnecessary suffering—simply by telling me the truth.

That is my desire for you. Whatever ordeal you might be experiencing, whatever disappointment you suffered yesterday or ten years ago, genuine hope can keep you moving forward. You will come through your trial. God's perfect love has been working throughout your life, and it will continue working in you until the end. He will cast out your fears (see 1 John 4:18) and release "the fullness of him who fills all in all" (Ephesians 1:23). That is the healing life He has planned for you. In Him, you can face every issue squarely, trusting Him to heal your broken places from the inside out.

Moving in Hope

When you are hurting, the word *process* can be infuriating. The idea that your solution might not be instantaneous can seem cruel and uncaring. You might want to shout, "But, Lord, I need it yesterday!"

Whatever you are suffering, a Band-Aid will not do. You don't want the issue covered up; you want it rooted out. You have come too far to settle for coping strategies and quick fixes. Let God's healing process prevail. Submit yourself to the grunt work of taking one step and then another and another, following Him all the while. He's not putting you through your paces for nothing. He is inviting you to partner with Him as He leads you into ever-increasing light.

Praying in Hope

Father, it is clear that what I learned about power as a child has not served me well: I learned that big people had it, and I didn't. Knowing that Your Holy Spirit dwells in me, I do not want to live as one who is disempowered. Help me to unlearn that lesson, surrender my avoidance patterns, and reclaim the power of Your indwelling Spirit, who causes me to triumph through Jesus and His cross. Thank You for Your healing, which occurs from the inside out and causes me to live the same way. In Jesus' name I pray. Amen.

DAY

16

The Human Condition

No testing has overtaken you that is not common to everyone. God is faithful, and he will not let you be tested beyond your strength, but with the testing he will also provide the way out so that you may be able to endure it.

1 Corinthians 10:13

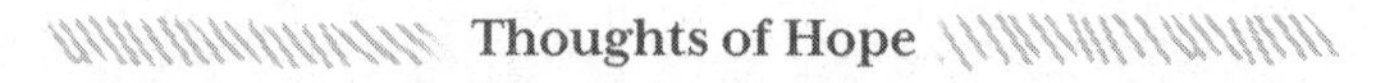

Thoughts of Hope

Human beings are said to have five basic fears.[1] The root of them all is the fear of death itself and of the act of dying. We Christians often distance ourselves from death altogether, as though our innate fear is unnatural or we are not afraid at all. But fear is a standard element of the human condition. And as far as I know, Christians are human, too.

The Creator does not ignore your fears. He knows your frame. The Scriptures encourage you not to be afraid for one reason: Fear inevitably comes. Not all of it is negative. Some fears are healthy and help you to make good decisions. In the extreme, the fear of breaking your neck keeps you from diving into an empty pool. The more basic fear of hurting a loved one helps you temper your words. Some of your fears are less rational, however. They are the ones that can control you and keep you from living a full life. But even those fears are real and worthy of your attention.

You can overcome painful, irrational fears by understanding how they work and what drives them. One of the conditions fear loves most is ignorance. When you ignore your fear, you unknowingly create the inner environment that helps it flourish. Instead of making your fear vanish, your disregard presses it deeper into your unconscious mind and allows it to fester undetected. You might seem at ease and in control. You might even believe that you are fearless. Then suddenly, a crisis comes, triggers the fear you buried, and turns your emotions upside down.

You might misunderstand your fear and try to shrug it off because of the "Do not fear" Scripture verses you have read (see Isaiah 41:10, 13–14; Joel 2:21; Matthew 10:31; John 12:15, etc.). Those instructions came to individuals in various situations, but they had nothing to do with living in denial. Instead, they encouraged an elevated perspective *in the face of fear*—a way of seeing fear in relation to the light of God's presence and power. It is a lot like what parents tell children who believe that monsters are hiding under their beds. Mommy or Daddy says, "Don't be afraid, baby, I'm here."

You can misunderstand in another way, by automatically distrusting secular disciplines like psychology and statistics. Many Christians do. But all truth is God's truth. Psychologists and statistics simply acknowledge what is already present in the human experience. That kind of information is not contrary to faith but can help you to know and care for yourself better. That is important, because if the powers of darkness know you better than you know yourself, they will use what you don't know to control you. That is part of what landed me in the darkest place I have ever known. Overcoming *that* misery was a lot harder than admitting my fear in the first place. Believe me, there is nothing blissful about being ignorant where your fear is concerned.

When you recognize your human susceptibility to fear or any other emotion, you are empowered to thrive in spite of it. Avoidance only puts you at odds with yourself. You know in your depths that you are not fearless because you know you are human. Yet you deny your fear—not because you are a liar but because you desperately want to cope and convince yourself that everything is okay. But, beloved, it never works. No one can make everything okay. As sure as the façade of control stands, it will eventually come down. Why not let it crumble and bring your fears to God in prayer? His love will cast them out (see 1 John 4:18).

Moving in Hope

If you are working hard to fight your fears, stop fighting. Simply acknowledge them and submit them to God, whose love and mercy are unending. Ask Him to expose the unconscious ways in which your fear operates. Let Him give you understanding and reveal His way of approaching fear, so you can learn and grow through it. Take heart, knowing that when the presence of fear no longer intimidates you, fear loses its power. And when you own what makes you afraid, the powers of darkness lose a prime foothold.

Praying in Hope

Father, I admit that my fears often get the best of me, and I fight them because they make me uncomfortable and restless. Yet fighting them does not make them go away. Help me to stop fighting them and start owning them, so I can fully surrender them to You. Grant me the grace to do that even now, as I depend on Jesus and the Spirit to deliver me. Break the deeply rooted chains that cause me to react in this way, so that these fears no longer rule or define me. In Jesus' name, amen.

DAY
17

Honest Answers

Who can hide in secret places so that I cannot see them? says the LORD. Do I not fill heaven and earth? says the LORD.

Jeremiah 23:24

Thoughts of Hope

Have you had your fill of easy answers? Are you weary of hearing "Fine, thanks" when you ask someone, "How are you today?" Do you wonder what *fine* means but know a pat answer when you hear one? Verbal shortcuts are easy ways for people to skirt their issues, hide their pain, and ignore their inadequacy in dealing with it.

Sometimes, people use shortcuts to answer *your* pain. You may have confessed that your heart is broken, only to hear, "Oh, you'll get over it." It's a pat answer. Yes, you will get over it, but that doesn't mean your heart isn't in pieces right now. The last thing you need is a bromide that glosses over your suffering and loss. A lot of well-meaning people tried to console me with pat answers to my complex and excruciating experience with anxiety. Often, they padded their answers with Scripture. The verses were true, but they were plucked out of context. It might have been better for them to say nothing at all.

Have you received that kind of input? Did the words seem empty, like clouds without water? Did a platitude leave you feeling dismissed and invisible? I learned early in my academic journey about the careful handling of Scripture and the difference between using proof texts and "rightly handling the word of truth" (2 Timothy 2:15 ESV). When you're hurting, overgeneralizations of Scripture leave you cold. You don't need someone to justify or prove a point. You need them to love you. In the end, proof texts cannot deliver what they seem to promise.

Beloved, you can take the same shortcuts all by yourself. Like those who disappoint you, you don't mean to do it, but sometimes you're at a loss for words. Like when you experience anxiety and read a verse like Philippians 4:6. You tell yourself to quit being anxious, because that's what Paul seems to be telling the Philippians: "Do not be anxious about anything." But what if your anxiety won't budge and you feel even more defeated than before? Was the verse still true? Yes. But was the application fitting? Maybe not.

Perhaps you are being physically abused, and you read Matthew 5:39. When your abuser "strikes you on the right cheek," should you "turn the other [cheek] also"? Is that what the verse is saying? Would Jesus tell you to submit to ongoing physical abuse? Would you expect someone else to embrace beatings on a continuing basis? Probably not, but the proof text seems to say something different.

When you are suffering, proof texts and other generalizations ring hollow and add to your anguish. They simply lack the grace and power of an honest, heartfelt answer. You cannot stop other people from painting over your struggles with substitutes, but you can stop doling them out to yourself. Don't condemn yourself. Just admit that you have taken verbal and emotional shortcuts. Acknowledge that the overwhelming experience of pain prompted you to respond that way. I believe that is what happened to the disciples who fell asleep while Jesus agonized at Gethsemane. They were devastated by what was happening and had no clue what to do or say. So they fell asleep.

If you let it, pain will lead you toward escape routes, shortcuts, and platitudes that you hope will cover over what you feel inadequate to address. Instead of shrinking back from reality and the emotions it evokes, seek honest answers for yourself and offer them to others, in love.

Moving in Hope

Whatever hurdle you are facing, speaking to it honestly is part of your healing journey. The apostle Paul did not mask his sufferings. He simply acknowledged them in plain, straightforward language. Look at what the great apostle wrote:

> I have labored and toiled and have often gone without sleep; I have known hunger and thirst and have often gone without food; I have been cold and naked. Besides everything else, I face daily the pressure of my concern for all the churches. Who is weak, and I do not feel weak? Who is led into sin, and I do not inwardly burn? If I must boast, I will boast of the things that show my weakness.
>
> 2 Corinthians 11:27–30 NIV

Let Paul's suffering remind you that, although you are not a first-century apostle, there is meaning and value in your suffering. No proof texting is necessary, and no platitudes need apply!

Praying in Hope

Father, at times I am guilty of oversimplifying what I read in Scripture. I fail to consider that what I really need is, first, to squarely face my afflictive emotions and pains and, second, to discover what is driving them. Help me to become more aware of my reliance on shortcuts and pat answers. Forgive me for wanting the Scripture to validate my less-than-accurate interpretations of Your intent. Teach me to draw from the sacred text only what the Spirit placed there. Slow me down to the speed of life and honesty, so I can embrace each opportunity to learn from my pain. In Jesus' name, amen.

DAY

18

The Accuser's Voice

Now have come the salvation and the power and the kingdom of our God and the authority of his Messiah, for the accuser of our brothers and sisters has been thrown down, who accuses them day and night before our God.

Revelation 12:10

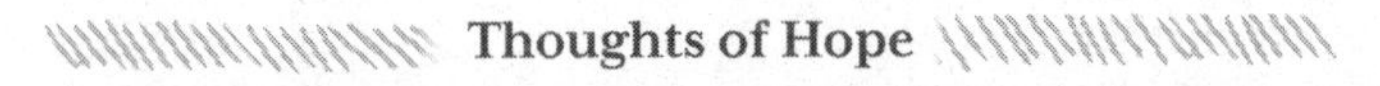

Thoughts of Hope

Today might be one of those days of feeling vulnerable—to life, regrets, or weaknesses. Maybe you are someone other people usually turn to for strength. You might be accustomed to lifting them up when everything in their world looks down. Now suddenly, you seem unable to be strong, and lifting your own head is more than you can manage.

The fact is that you *are* vulnerable. Every human being is. And if your season is an especially difficult one, you might find many reasons to feel that way. But don't be too quick to embrace those reasons. The enemy of your soul is the ultimate opportunist. He takes great pleasure in your pain and in daring you to heal yourself (knowing you can't). He relishes your sense of vulnerability even more than the vulnerability itself. Day and night, he will remind you of your difficulty and emphasize your hurdles. He will try to drive a wedge between you and God, tempting you to distrust God, the way he tempted Job. The accuser will not hesitate to spew accusations through the people around you, which he also did in Job's case.

Beloved, listen for the voice of your Redeemer, but discern the voice of your accuser, too. The Lord will help you elevate your thoughts, but the accuser will turn your thoughts against you. The Lord's words will soothe your wounds, but the accuser's words will add insult to your injury. The Lord will keep leading you to an open place, but the accuser will claim that your open places are behind you now, as though there were no redemption or refuge ahead. He never mentions God's mercy. Why would he? And perhaps that is the most telltale sign of his accusatory voice.

In your dark wood, the accuser will surely speak. After all, he tempted even Jesus in His wilderness and tried to derail the divine intent of God and His Christ. You are Christ's. Will not the accuser try to distract you? He surely will! He will tell you that you are not equipped or prepared to come through this trial. He will say that you lack the physical, emotional, and spiritual resources to weather the storm. But there is a fallacy in his argument: No matter how plentiful or scant your resources are, they are not enough. You cannot set yourself free with wealth or willpower or anything else that you can muster. By design, you are dependent upon God; *He* is your source.

That can be the greatest lesson of your dark season. You are not a free agent created to fend for yourself. You are Christ's! Your dependency on Him is not a weakness but a strength. He is your provision, your life, and your breath. He is your defender and your wisdom, your righteousness and sanctification. Don't expect the accuser to remind you of these truths. Don't wait for him to mention that your deliverance comes not by fighting your pain or rebuking the powers of darkness, but in your willingness to rest in God. Why would he reveal the riches from which he is excluded?

You are not excluded, however. You can trust the Lord and follow Him, even in the utter nakedness of your faith, knowing that your faith is all you have to offer. Your Father is satisfied with that. You can trust Him to be with you in the darkness. You can know that even when you see no signs that your ordeal is ending, your Deliverer is with you, and your deliverance is with Him.

Moving in Hope

During Job's dark season, the accuser tried relentlessly to crush his hopes. Not only did he accuse Job before God, but he sent Job's friends to accuse him to his face. In the midst of almost unimaginable suffering, Job endured the slander, kept his pain in perspective, and continued to praise and worship God. Job defied the accuser, not by arguing with him or portraying fearlessness, but by being transparent in his suffering and affirming his trust in his Creator.

When the accuser rehashes your mess and reminds you of how dark your darkness is, take your rest and worship your God. The accuser might be relentless, but so is your King.

Praying in Hope

Father, I have allowed the accuser to harass me and make me despondent more times than I care to count. When I fall prey to accusation, cause me to discern it more quickly, even when it is concealed in questions that are designed to gnaw at my well-being. When I forget, please remind me to take up the shield of faith by which I will extinguish all the fiery darts the accuser hurls at me. Strengthen me to take the sword of the Spirit—Your Word—to my lips, and talk back, renouncing aloud all the devil's lies. In Jesus' name, amen.

DAY

19

Fully Awake

> Everything exposed by the light becomes visible, for everything that becomes visible is light. Therefore it says, "Sleeper, awake! Rise from the dead, and Christ will shine on you."
>
> Ephesians 5:13–14

Thoughts of Hope

Acceptance starts the healing journey that leads to being fully awake. You can be conscious, yet not yet awakened to your patterned responses. You can feel alert yet react to events by force of habit. The reason your unconscious patterns persist is obvious: You are not conscious of them. But as you awaken, you become aware of how you see the world, interpret your experiences, and respond to them.

Beloved, to be fully awake is to be fully alive. But it does not happen by accident. You awaken as you face your thoughts and actions honestly and own them. Instead of living reflexively, you live purposefully, from the inside out. This exposes your avoidance strategies so you can see them and discard them. You realize that despite any momentary relief they might offer, they only deepen and prolong your pain. So you exchange short-term comfort for long-term peace. Your healing begins to manifest as your ways of observing and interpreting life are renewed.

Living from the inside out is a key to becoming fully human. It is how you were designed to live—as an embodied spirit, unified, integrated, self-aware, and others-aware. It is a lifelong journey, a process of becoming increasingly whole, and it continues until you are in your resurrected body. In today's culture and even much of the Church, this process is often overlooked. You may have lost sight of it yourself. Yet you also sense the fragmentation that plagues us all. You might even have been taught that your "good" spirit is trapped in an "evil" body. That is a misunderstanding of the truth. Your body does experience corruption because of Adam's sin, but your body is not evil. You simply live in a fallen world where your body takes a beating from environmental, emotional, economic, social, and other factors.

If you are like most twenty-first-century people, you can also be tempted to abuse your body and burden it with unhealthy demands. Are popular views of success, performance, and perfection driving you? Are you telling yourself that God's call demands you to be driven? If so, you will be prone to ignoring your physical self-abuse or accepting it as a fair price to pay for serving Him. There is so much more that I could say about this. But let me simply assure you that God has not asked you to ignore the health of your body or your mind.

Be aware that when your drive to succeed is combined with free-floating anxiety, the temptation to ignore your body's warnings will increase. Pay attention and become more an observer than a reactor. Instead of compartmentalizing your life so you can avoid paying attention, allow yourself to become fully awake, so you can acknowledge the red flags your body raises. Over time, you will develop the emotional intelligence to respond appropriately. Without it, you will unwittingly put yourself in a vulnerable position and become more susceptible to whatever adversity or confusion comes down the pike.

Are you sensing your need to hear this? Have you lived with your foot on the accelerator, attempting to "make it happen"? Perhaps the negative effects of your lifestyle are becoming more evident each day. The "little" things you thought you could ignore might seem more pronounced than they once did. Heed them! They are not your enemies, but messengers inviting you to fully awaken and come to yourself. If, by the Spirit, you listen, you will make room for wholeness, which is exactly what you crave. After all, you were not created to sleepwalk through your life. You were built to embrace it, fully awake and fully alive.

Moving in Hope

It seems strange, but it's true: We seek ways to stay asleep. We do it through unconscious patterns of avoidance that we develop to help us cope. They are variations on the "what I don't know won't hurt me" theme. We continually put the issues we'd like to avoid on the back burner. Then the pot spills over, and we are forced to wake up.

Being awake is best in the long run. It's infinitely easier to recognize your contrary patterns and deal with them than it is to ignore them. Don't pressure yourself into an overnight transformation, however. And don't take on everything at once. Your steady, incremental steps will lead you toward freedom.

Praying in Hope

All too often, Father, I have numbed out the strains and stresses that accumulate in my body and failed to remember that I am an embodied soul. My body feels every external stress that I withstand and registers all the internal stresses that result from thoughts I hold on to. Thank You for teaching me how to slow down and listen to my body, while giving it the space needed to recover during the tough times. You indeed quicken my mortal body as I awaken to Your indwelling Spirit, who raises me out of dead things and into Your life. In Jesus' name, amen.

DAY

20

The Healing Cycle

> For everything there is a season and a time for every matter under heaven: . . . a time to plant and a time to pluck up what is planted; . . . a time to seek and a time to lose; a time to keep and a time to throw away; a time to tear and a time to sew.
>
> Ecclesiastes 3:1–2, 6–7

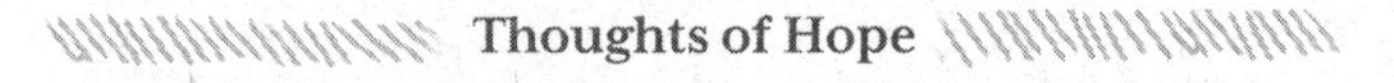

Thoughts of Hope

You are called to a healing life that consists of many seasons and cycles of healing. Some will be swift and easy to bear. Others will progress slowly and try your patience. Sometimes, matters will seem to get worse before they get better. Either way, your wholeness will require more than a prayer and an easy fix. The healing cycle begs your faith and your presence in the *now* moment.

Are you on a healing journey? Is it hard to admit that you are suffering and need to be healed? I understand. Whether you are suffering with a chronic physical ailment or a psychological issue such as anxiety or depression, you naturally want the healing cycle to be quick. If it doesn't run its course "soon enough," you can become discouraged. Limitations are hard to accept, and the frustration they trigger is real. There is no button you can press to fix everything. And even if you do everything you are supposed to do exactly right, you cannot control the healing process.

I learned that lesson! I had to admit that I could not control my healing "schedule." I could cooperate with it, but it was not fully in my hands. The issues underlying my anxiety also contributed to delays. My healing could not be complete until I became conscious of them. For me, that process was difficult. I had buried certain deep-seated beliefs and assumptions that set up my anxiety in the first place. Those thought systems did not develop overnight, and they would not come down by morning. I had to see them as they were and acknowledge them. That meant getting to know myself better and understanding how I related to my environment and to people in that environment. As I learned, I became open to seeing life differently. I began to heal!

By design, you are a meaning-maker. You take in everything around you and everything you experience, and without consciously thinking about it, you interpret it, continually. In a sense, you are taking notes and storing them in your psyche. As a living, breathing, walking set of interpretations, you carry your interpretations with you *every place you go*. They determine how you see yourself, life, and other people. They determine whether you view events in a positive or negative light. They even affect your ability to appreciate life's blessings.

Beloved, the cycle of healing affects your ability to live from the inside out. I know success gurus try to make that sound easy, but it is more complicated than they let on. Your path to healing might be less straight than you would choose. More often than not, it includes unexpected twists and turns that seem like deviations but are really important parts of your self-discovery.

Are you discouraged by the healing cycle you are in? Do you feel like it's going nowhere fast? Take heart. Give yourself the grace to keep going, knowing that certain pains are being worked out in the process. Allow for your self-awareness to increase day by day. Be patient as your observations and interpretations of reality are progressively healed. You have waited too long to quit now. What you want and need is to respond to life in integrated ways. So trust the process and complete it. You and your future are worth the wait.

Moving in Hope

The inescapable fact is that healing requires you to face your issues squarely. You cannot do that unless you develop the self-awareness that allows you to see yourself clearly and face issues honestly. That kind of healing takes time. Don't feel cheated; see the time as an investment in your well-being. After all, what you really want is not temporary relief from your pain but the sustainable state of well-being that allows for a joyful, peaceful life.

Cooperate with the cycle of healing and trust the Healer to be present. Allow Him to have His way and heal you from the inside out. You are His child, and healing is the children's bread (see Matthew 15:22–28).

Praying in Hope

Father, I thank You for leading me on this healing journey. I am grateful to be moving forward in spite of the temporary setbacks I experience. Your Spirit is causing me to be enlarged from the inside out, even during the most distressing and difficult challenges. Thank You for helping me to be patient and present in the moment, so I can learn and grow along the way. I affirm that Your Son can live large in me as I make room for Him. I acknowledge and affirm what You are doing in and through me as I cooperate with Your indwelling Spirit. In Jesus' name, amen.

DAY 21

In the Mercy of God

> He saved us, not because of any works of righteousness that we had done, but according to his mercy, through the water of rebirth and renewal by the Holy Spirit.
>
> Titus 3:5

Thoughts of Hope

Has this morning already drained you, and it's only nine o'clock? Have you navigated a long day and discovered at midnight that sleep is the farthest thing from your mind? Every adult has been there. Some days, there seems to be too much to do and too little time to do it. Financial strains or strife can complicate matters, and workplace dynamics can wear you out.

At other times, it's harder to pinpoint what the trouble is. When that happens, there could be something "new" breaking into your conscious awareness. Discomfiting trends such as restlessness, anxiety, or sadness can flood to the forefront for no apparent reason. But because they make you uneasy, they get your attention. This conscious awareness might seem disruptive, but it is a positive step in recognizing issues or aspects of issues that have previously flown under your radar.

When your unfinished business refuses to stay buried, fear can seem to pull you toward the edge of darkness and unleash an almost suffocating form of free-floating anxiety. Suddenly, it seems like nothing is right, and everything looks wrong. But that might not be exactly the case. When what you buried alive rises to the surface of your consciousness, you can move in the direction of healing and greater peace. What looks like the edge of darkness becomes the edge of hope.

Are you there now? I know that place well, and I know how hard it is to admit to yourself or anyone else that you are troubled in ways you cannot explain. Yet that is your way forward. Healing begins when you acknowledge your need of it, and in God's economy, that usually involves other people.

You have covered some of that ground in previous devotions, but there is another benefit of accepting where you are and allowing others to be part of your journey: It thwarts the concerted efforts of the powers of darkness to isolate you. They are skilled in using your fears and silence to drive your pain deeper and afflict you even more. They are skilled in separating you from the very people God has placed in your life. The powers are merciless!

Ah, but God! Amid your discomfort and fears, He remains steadfast and ever present. Whether you are consciously aware of it or not, He is working in you. When the powers of darkness prophesy your defeat, the God of angel armies has the last word. When your situation seems utterly hopeless, when your strength and resources are already expended, when there seems to be no way forward and no place good to which you can return, you are not at the mercy of any force or circumstance. You are deep in the mercy of God.

In His seamless way, God works below the level of your consciousness—the very place where your fear and anxiety have been brewing. He hears every one of your prayers. He has heard your unspoken cries. He has neither left nor forsaken you. Yes, He might have allowed certain difficulties to unfold, but even those experiences are within the scope of His mercy. He knows what the forces of darkness refuse to acknowledge—that your ordeal can reveal the edge of hope, the liminal, life-transforming place where God works in and through everything for your good.

Let the most high God do for your weary soul what only He can do. No matter what trouble you face, He knew the end of it before you even realized it had begun. He had every situation in hand before it came to your conscious awareness. He guarded you even in your fitful sleep. He is not seeking to "fix" you or have you "fix" yourself. You are not a machine but a living soul made in His image and likeness. Allow Him to restore your soul and renew your hope. Let Him lead you through your fears and anxiety and into the green pastures where you are healed and made whole.

Moving in Hope

To be a sinner saved by grace is to be rescued from the pit and from destruction. You might feel pressured by battles on every front. It might seem as though your defenses are giving way, and you are at the mercy of the merciless. Your perceptions are understandably laced with pain, but they are only part of the story.

In this life, there is a brokenness that only God can remedy. You cannot wage war against it or defeat it with the "right" words or level of determination. But in Him is your ability to overcome. Tell Him the very things you are afraid to acknowledge. He cannot heal what you conceal, so lay it all bare before Him, and let His mercy cover you.

Praying in Hope

Father, I thank You that in Christ I am more than a conqueror. Please continue to quicken the areas of my consciousness that need to reawaken. Help me to cooperate with You and be strengthened to do all things. You will indeed enlarge my footsteps under me and set my feet in a large place. You will lead me in a plain path because of my enemies. Take heed of the accusations and pushback I face. When I am drained, please renew my strength in Jesus! When I am assailed, crush the enemy under my feet! In Jesus' name, amen.

DAY

22

Being and Becoming

> It is no longer I who live, but it is Christ who lives in me. And the life I now live in the flesh I live by the faith of the Son of God, who loved me and gave himself for me.
>
> Galatians 2:20

Thoughts of Hope

Regrets. Every living soul has them. They are tied to the past, but you experience them in the present. They tell you that everything you have been and experienced make up the sum total of who you are, as though you had already reached your end point and had nowhere left to turn or go. But like all perceptions, they are interpretations of what you observe, and they are colored by the feelings, emotions, experiences, and other factors that frame your way of seeing.

At best, what you perceive is incomplete. Often, the piece that is still missing is the reality of what is yet to come. Who you are involves your past and your present. But who you are becoming is about your future. That involves what you know so far and what you can imagine. Your dark wood is not a figment of your imagination. It has already manifested in real time, with real consequences. But God has gifted you with your imagination and intuition. That means you can see your future differently. By His design, you have the cognitive ability to envision what *can be*.

You are not doomed to endlessly repeat the known past. You are empowered to perceive a path beyond where you are and who you are now. With your sanctified imagination, you can envision the person you will become in a future that is otherwise unknown. But why a *sanctified* imagination? It is simply because human imaginations don't always reflect the light of the divine. With your sanctified imagination, however, you choose that which is and *can be* in Christ. In Him you are not confined to what seems to be true. You are liberated to grasp what is most real—not according to the limitations you perceive, but according to the limitless goodness of the omnipotent God. When you envision what is real *despite* what seems to be, you can become something greater than what you have been. You can go somewhere greater than you have experienced so far. And you can leave behind something far greater than you once believed possible.

Beloved, you are not stuck in the precedents that have marked your life. Even in your darkest seasons, you are both being and becoming. You are more than the sum total of your thoughts, feelings, and actions to date. They are largely the story of the past, and you have not been sentenced to repeat it! The rest of your story—perhaps the greatest chapter so far—is still ahead. However sunny or gray the current moment is, the rest of your story lives in the will of God and in your ability to imagine what can be.

Is your imagination currently bogged down by anxiety and worst-case scenarios? Maybe you feel unable to see your history in any but the worst possible light. The school of hard knocks may have taught you that things will only get worse, and change is no longer possible. Chances are you don't feel "up to" the task of changing anyway. It might seem as though your thoughts have you, and not the other way around.

Fret not! Keep turning to God, even when you believe your prayers are not rising above the level of your ceiling. Let Him lift the burdens you have struggled to carry. Let Him heal what you realize you cannot fix. Simply rest in the idea that your *being and becoming* are not matters of self-effort but of God's own grace and timing. It is no longer that you live but that Christ lives in you. You are not stuck within your own limits; you are free to live by the faith of the Son of God!

Moving in Hope

The more unconsciously you live, the less aware you are of this transforming truth: You can choose how you see yourself and your life experiences. If you change nothing about how you see reality, nothing else will change. So even before you pray for God to change your circumstances, ask Him to adjust your way of seeing them. Ask Him to reveal the unconscious thought patterns that keep you repeating the known past. When that change comes, you will feel free to envision a different kind of future and *enter it*.

This is what God is offering. Why not take Him up on it?

Praying in Hope

Father, You are calling me to a wider, more expansive future in which the greater potential that lies within me can be more fully realized. I have no desire to live in places that are too small and limiting. I have done that for too long. Instead, I choose to believe that You are taking me up higher and ever deeper into the life of union with Your Son, where I share in His nature and partake of His many blessings. From there, I cry out with a loud voice, "You are setting me free!" In Jesus' name, amen.

DAY
23

Living in Your Body

> I appeal to you therefore, brothers and sisters, on the basis of God's mercy, to present your bodies as a living sacrifice, holy and acceptable to God, which is your reasonable act of worship. Do not be conformed to this age, but be transformed by the renewing of the mind, so that you may discern what is the will of God—what is good and acceptable and perfect.
>
> Romans 12:1–2

Thoughts of Hope

Beloved, by divine design you are an embodied spirit—an integrated being who can think, feel, worship, speak, and act all at the same time. Your consciousness and bodily systems are connected. Your mental and physical states function in concert. Your emotions can be expressed as physical pain, and your physical pain affects your emotions. You are a holistic being whose cells communicate with one another.

Even so, you can learn to live in your head, as though you were literally cut off from your body. This disorienting way of life leaves you feeling dissociated from yourself. Being in such a state obscures things that are obvious, so that your agitation and anxiety get no attention. But your agitation can be a sign of exhaustion, and your anxiety can be your body's way of alerting you to the stress and emotions you have been burying for too long.

Are you tired of being tired? Have you felt that way for longer than you can remember? I understand the drive to "keep on keepin' on." It can become a badge of honor that says, "Hey, world, look at all I can handle!" All of us have tried wearing that badge. May the Lord forgive us and help us to see the error of our ways. Running hard 24/7/365 does not earn us achievement awards in heaven. We may have been taught to treat our bodies like machines, but not by God.

We are not machines, and even machines break down. Because life's demands never seem to quit, we book ourselves wall to wall with commitments that seem compulsory but really aren't. Even our children are booked solid with after-school and weekend events and teams. We are geared toward speed and continual activity. Cell phones keep us wired morning, noon, and night. We tell ourselves that job security isn't what it used to be, so we have to go, go, go.

In Day 2, I mentioned the mistaken belief that human feelings undermine faith, because the flesh is essentially evil and opposes God. Theologically, the idea is at odds even with the incarnation. The God who created and loves you has not asked you to denigrate the body or the physical feelings He gave you. To ask that would be to violate both His design and His love. Would He ask you to dissociate from yourself and reality? No. He gave you a body to function according to His wisdom, and you use that body to serve Him. It is the "living sacrifice" you present as your "reasonable act of worship," and it speaks through your feelings.

Listening to what you feel in your body is not a sin. When your body warns that you have overstepped your bounds, make whatever adjustments you need to make. When it tells you that your nutrition could be better, then improve your eating habits. Is your exhaustion speaking to you? Are you loading up on vitamins and caffeine but still feel like you have to drag yourself through each day? Your body is telling you the truth. You may be spreading yourself too thin, trying to be everything to everybody. Maybe you are suffering from sleep deprivation and the continual stress of an overwhelming schedule. Either one will exact a cost that your vitamins and fitness level cannot cover.

Live in your body. Don't worship it, but honor and care for it. It's the only one you've got, and it is the temple that houses the sacred presence of the Lord.

Moving in Hope

Distrusting your feelings can only frustrate the Spirit's work in you. Remember that you are not a compartmentalized being, and God has not called you to disregard any part of yourself. He created you to function as an integrated whole. That is apparent in Romans 12. Meditate on Paul's appeal for mercy, which was predicated on what the Roman Christians did with their bodies. According to Paul, their minds were renewed as they offered their bodies, not as they ignored them! Take this truth to heart today and be thankful that your body speaks to you.

Praying in Hope

Father, forgive me for not recognizing the integrated nature of my being. I repent for not paying attention when my body is out of sorts. My body has faithfully kept an account of my stressors, emotions, and ways of seeing the world. In this season, I am ready to listen to my body and care for it in a more meaningful way. Help me to be consciously present to the body You gave me, always presenting it as a living example of my continuing surrender to Your love, grace, care, and power. May this be a season of new beginnings, in Jesus' name!

DAY
24

Friendship

> Some friends play at friendship, but a true friend sticks closer than one's sibling.
>
> Proverbs 18:24

Thoughts of Hope

When you are "hoping against hope" (Romans 4:18), you want to hear from God, but hearing can seem difficult. You want to be still and know that He is God (see Psalm 46:10), but it is often easier said than done. Even if you have lived your whole adult life trusting Him, you can feel cut off, as though you cannot return to yourself or to His presence.

God has not cut you off, but I understand the feeling, and I know how painful it is. There seems to be no place of refuge, stillness, or rest. The more you long for them, the more they evade your grasp. You begin to wonder whether you will ever experience them again. And when you feel anxious, your wondering can turn into despair. Amid the chaos, even the promises of God can sound like taunts that tease and provoke you.

When your mind is racing day and night, your strength withers and God's voice can seem distant. Under the strain, your emotions can become almost overwhelming. You might even think that you are going out of your mind. In those moments, the temptation to isolate yourself comes calling. It is hard to invite people into your chaos. You don't want to be seen when you are at your worst. No one does. So although you feel like you are coming undone and desperately need reassurance, you retreat to the cover of darkness, which seems like a safer approach.

Beloved, the worst time to self-isolate is when you feel utterly alone and miles from God. Part of the temptation to disappear is based in shame. Imagine being ashamed because you are in terrible pain! My wife and I love our dogs. When they are suffering, they let us know. They are not ashamed to be hurting, and we are not ashamed of them. In fact, we are heartbroken over their suffering and ready to pray and provide whatever care they need to recover. *How much more does God long to care for His children?* Yet when I was suffering, I shrank back and sat in the dark for hours. Any sense of shame I felt over my severe anxiety only made it harder to bear. More importantly, the shame was not godly in the least. It was demonic!

You already know about my precious friend Vinnie. If any man or woman ever modeled friendship in its full flower, it was Vinnie. He has since passed on into glory, but the way he loved people brought some of God's glory to this earth.

His love was unconditional and truly life-giving. To say he was a friend who stood closer than a brother does not even approximate what he did. With Vinnie I could be transparent. When I could not hear God's voice, I heard God speak through Vinnie. When I forgot who I was in Christ, Vinnie reminded me. And when he traveled with me, he was willing to walk the floor with me all night long.

If you are suffering terribly, find your Vinnie, someone whose compassion and care will help you see your way forward. That someone will help you rediscover God's promises. God will use your Vinnie to revive your hope and break the tension when your torment is so severe that you despair of life itself. Someone in your life can remind you how to smile and laugh. And yes, your Vinnie can handle your pain, not with platitudes but with his or her presence. It won't matter how raw your anguish is or how long it lasts. Your Vinnie will see you through and listen to your complaints, not the way Job's friends did, but with the pure heart that longs for your restoration as much as you do.

If you are suffering in any way, come out of your isolation. If you feel vulnerable doing it, do it anyway. Allow the right friend to serve as the healing presence of Christ, and His presence will reach you right where you are.

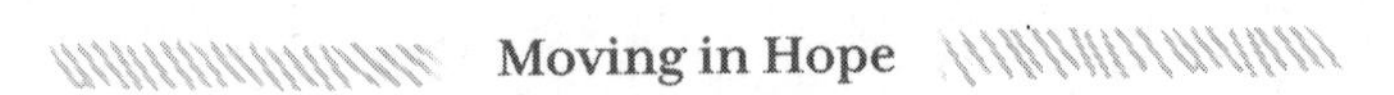

Moving in Hope

A God-sent friend can help you to be open and transparent when you would rather clam up and sit in the dark. Such a friend will not silence you or curb your complaints but encourage you to find your voice in your pain. Let someone perceive the layers of distress that are robbing your well-being. Let that person reach through your deepest silence and draw you toward the light.

Job's friends could have done this for him, but they chose to search out his sin instead. Your Vinnie will look for *you* in whatever hell you are going through. Finding such a friend is like finding an oasis, a clearing and room to breathe in your desert. Such a friend is priceless.

Praying in Hope

Father, I so easily withdraw and isolate myself when it seems like my only option. I have heard the voices of friends offering me their love and care. Yet I easily succumb to the chaos around me and the lie that says their presence won't make a difference. So I have learned to tune them out. Forgive me! You said that it isn't good for me to be alone, and I agree with You. Thank You for the friends You have given me as gifts. I am grateful and will receive them more freely in this season. In Jesus' name, amen.

DAY

25

God's Penetrating Gaze

> Indeed, the word of God is living and active and sharper than any two-edged sword, piercing until it divides soul from spirit, joints from marrow; it is able to judge the thoughts and intentions of the heart.
>
> Hebrews 4:12

Thoughts of Hope

Where can you go and escape Christ's gaze? The answer is nowhere. And how far does His gaze reach? It reaches as far as your deepest depths. Whatever Christ says concerning you—whether He is speaking to you, about you, or over you—will penetrate your being and speak to your wounds. Regardless of what you are facing, His gaze can penetrate your secret recesses. He will shed His light, not only on what can be seen but also on what is hidden.

Hebrews 4:12 says that "the word of God is living and active and sharper than any two-edged sword." The writer to the Hebrews is speaking of the living Word, which is Christ. The same is true of these words from Isaiah 55:11 (NKJV): "So shall My word be that goes forth from My mouth; It shall not return to Me void, but it shall accomplish what I please, and it shall prosper in the thing for which I sent it." The living Word cannot be thwarted or overcome. Everything He says is supremely alive and powerful and able to accomplish whatever is in the divine will, so that what He *says* ultimately *does* what He is.

How glorious is that, especially in your dark night of the soul! When your life seems devoid of comfort, you can take comfort, knowing that regardless of the hell that has broken loose around you, His gaze will penetrate it. The living Word misses absolutely nothing. Every aspect of your life and every detail of your anguish is open to His sight. He sees every doubt and bears witness to every injustice you have suffered. He knows all that has befallen you. The One who is faithful and just sees *everything* that concerns or affects you.

Remember, however, that the sword with two edges cuts both ways, and with surgical precision. "No creature is hidden, but all are naked and laid bare to the eyes of the one to whom we must render an account" (Hebrews 4:13). During my darkest days, I could not escape my need of the divine surgeon. It took time for me to understand what I needed, but I eventually submitted to the "operation." Gradually, I became more open to God's way of healing me, but I was not necessarily at ease with the procedure, which proved radical. His penetrating gaze cut cleanly and deeply into the areas of my interiority that begged for His attention. At first, I did not understand what He was doing, especially because I felt worse before I felt better. I sometimes wished that He would just take me home. Nevertheless, His intense work in me brought the healing I desired, and much more than I could have asked.

Did I enjoy the process? Not really. But I can honestly say that I would not change a thing. His scalpel was not the instrument I would have chosen, but it was precisely what my condition required. He knew exactly what I needed in every harrowing moment. His gaze penetrated my inmost parts, always keeping in mind His intention for me. Sharp as His scalpel was, He guided it with love and mercy. He cut with precision, making a way out of my darkness and back into His marvelous light. His healing touch is matchless!

Beloved, the One who keeps you understands your fear of "going under the knife." He comes to your aid knowing about your every worry and fear. You might not enjoy the process, and He knows that. But you can trust Him and embrace His ways, despite your doubts. Allow His gaze to penetrate the tangled places in your life. Trust Him through your pain and let Him lift you above its reach. Neither your suffering nor His surgery are convenient. Yet avoiding them cannot help you. Let His penetrating gaze find you willing, so when the surgery is done, your thanksgiving will testify of His goodness.

Moving in Hope

The all-seeing God exposes every hidden thing to His scrutiny. In your darkest moments, when everything seems to be falling apart, you will want to postpone your "surgery." Incisions, even those God makes in your depths, can be intimidating. They take time to heal, and they require care. Yet there is no more opportune time for God's penetrating gaze to heal you. It is in your dark wood that His scalpel attends to your pain. You will be tempted to recoil, but you can resist the temptation. You can trust the living Word to *life you*.

Praying in Hope

Father, You have surrounded me behind and before. You see all I am and all I need. There is nowhere I can go or be that You are not already there, watching over me. Your Word is a lamp to my feet and a light to my path, especially in the dark places. You have prepared me to pay attention and allow the quality of my attention to be drawn toward Jesus and Your Good Spirit. I surrender to You my way of seeing, so that with Spirit-eyes, I can see what You, in Your profound love, want me to see. In Jesus' name, amen.

DAY
26

God in Your Depths

O Lord, you have searched me and known me. You know when I sit down and when I rise up; you discern my thoughts from far away. You search out my path and my lying down and are acquainted with all my ways. Even before a word is on my tongue, O Lord, you know it completely.

Psalm 139:1–4

Thoughts of Hope

Being open to God's penetrating gaze is a powerful move toward wholeness in which being seen and looking inward work together. Yet when your life seems out of joint and you need answers, you can become overly preoccupied with looking inward. The pressure can convince you that something is wrong with you and tempt you to dig up the soil of your heart to find it.

Looking inward *is* part of the healing process. But when it becomes a finger-pointing expedition or "manhunt" for the offender within, it is no longer about healing but about accusation and blame. The lover of your soul is not in the accusing business. He is in the healing business. His correction and discipline—yes, even His judgments—are part and parcel of His mercy. When He searches your heart, you can trust His gentleness. He will locate the triggers of your unrest, but His surgery is not only about removing what needs to go. It is also about resuscitating the precious parts of your heart, including the hopeful, creative places that have lain dormant under the weight of oppression and disappointment. He will awaken you to the living soul you were becoming and were created to be—the you who became hidden from sight over the course of time.

Beloved, God not only plumbs your depths; He is *in* your depths. Nothing that is hidden there comes as a surprise to Him. His gaze is not a threat but an assurance of His presence and love. You need not feel threatened by anything He does or plans to do in you. If you will set aside your urge to retreat from His watchful eye, you will find the courage to cooperate with the inner work that only He can do. When He lays bare the truth, He sheds light on your personhood and your very identity in Christ. In other words, He not only heals you but empowers you to live well.

Your dark night of the soul feels like a setup for your destruction, but that is only part of the story God is writing. Your dark days don't just come along and quietly fade away. They raise an emotional ruckus and demand your attention. Like I did, you might want to ignore them and hope they blow over. But if the season is dark enough, you won't have that option. Your struggle will commandeer your attention. And even if you could turn away, you would live to regret missing the opportunity for the God who is spirit to expose your depths and heal your pain at its roots.

Throughout his life, David entered seasons of travail and danger. At such times, he was compelled to look up and look in. He opened himself—warts and all—to the penetrating gaze of God's Spirit. As a psalmist, David articulated the sense of God in his depths in words that spoke from firsthand experience. He wrote, "You hem me in, behind and before, and lay your hand upon me. Such knowledge is too wonderful for me; it is so high that I cannot attain it. Where can I go from your spirit? Or where can I flee from your presence?" (Psalm 139:5–7).

Too wonderful indeed! Wherever you are, the God of the universe is there. Whatever you suffer, the God of Abraham, Isaac, and Jacob knows and is ready to comfort, guide, and restore you. Regardless of your self-doubts and wrongdoing, He is always tender, always patient. You cannot flee from His presence, but through a lack of attention or trust, you can forgo the healing touch that He offers. Will you pass it up or embrace Him in your depths?

Moving in Hope

Does turmoil leave you feeling "less than" as a human being and follower of Christ? In the presence of inescapable imperfection, you can succumb to a very human reflex and keep your depths hidden from view. But as you continue maturing in Christ, you learn that your cover-ups cannot produce good outcomes. And they surely cannot hide anything from the One who is acquainted with all your ways.

There are things you do not yet know about yourself. Whatever your age, you haven't got *you* all figured out. But the One who created you knows where your habits, pains, and frustrations are buried. Let Him do the digging and heal you.

Praying in Hope

Father, You know me better than I will ever know myself. For too long, I've allowed my introspection to make me susceptible to the accuser. I have easily forgotten that You love and care for me unconditionally. Remind me that You go before me and are my rear guard, You know when I sit down and rise up, You know my thoughts from afar, and You know my words before I utter them. Remind me as well that You're working all things for my good and Your glory, as You have called me for Your glorious eternal purpose. In Christ's name, amen.

DAY

27

Come, Complaints and All

With my voice I cry to the LORD; with my voice I make supplication to the LORD. I pour out my complaint before him; I tell my trouble before him. When my spirit is faint, you know my way. . . . I cry to you, O Lord; I say, "You are my refuge, my portion in the land of the living." Listen to my cry, for I am brought very low.

Psalm 142:1–3, 5–6

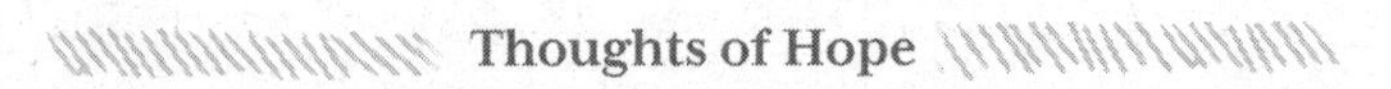

Thoughts of Hope

Complaining has gotten a bad name. Nobody enjoys chronic complainers, and whining is just not the Christian thing to do. Far be it from me to recommend griping as a way of life. Doing it for its own sake will keep you simmering in self-pity and the idea that you have nothing for which to be grateful. But that doesn't mean you should stuff every complaint behind a stiff upper lip.

Complaints have their place. If you are suffering, you know just how real your trouble is and every complication it has introduced into your life. Even if you are not suffering in this moment, you can remember times when the world seemed to collapse around you. You also know that at some point before you depart this life, you will experience another struggle. One of your greatest challenges will be to keep a clear head in the midst of it.

When your emotions are stirred and your circumstances seem jumbled, keeping a clear head is not so easy to do. With peril converging from every corner of your life, your thoughts can go haywire. Should you deny them? No. Your reactions may be raw, but they are coming from the heart of your pain. You cannot deny that they exist. In fact, for the sake of your mental well-being, you need to acknowledge them. But then what? Should you "just get over it" and put your complaints in storage? Should you sanitize them and share them with a trusted friend? Or should you blurt them out, unfiltered and unreserved before God?

You might be grappling with this very question today. You want to be clearheaded, but the lines are blurring as the pressure within you builds. You don't want to air your dirty laundry, but in your pain, you sense that a crescendo is coming, and something is going to give. You also know that it won't help in the long run to maintain misplaced notions of faith that forbid emotional honesty about just how awful you feel.

There is a sound way forward: Simply face your emotions and feelings honestly and take every bit of your mess to God, however uncut and unprocessed it is. You did not come this far without realizing that He knows your every thought before you see it coming. So why try to conceal your unrest? He knows about your anger before it erupts and hears every snarky word that leaps out of your mouth. You might as well take the load off your shoulders and lay it before Him. Instead of hiding from Him, come, and let Him minister to you!

Your next-door neighbor might not want to hear your complaints, but your High Priest understands them. To filter them from your conversation with Him would be like trying to dress up your insides with a fig leaf. Why not be real and commune with the One who is touched with the feeling of your infirmity (see Hebrews 4:15 KJV)? There is nothing you can feel or endure that Jesus did not experience on the cross. He knows exactly where your emotions are, and He knows how to sort them out and bring them into balance.

How else can you be healed? Can you run to Jesus and leave your brokenness, trauma, and regrets outside the gate? He is big enough to handle them. He is not insulted or drained by your lack of composure. So let Him hear your heart, complaints and all.

Moving in Hope

When your troubles seem too great to bear, voicing your complaint to God is the most honest and faithful thing you can do. Isn't that what the psalmists did? Have you not noticed how raw their emotions were? And what about Job? He was clearheaded where his faith in God was concerned, but he was dead honest about his inner chaos. He poured out to God everything that he felt and feared. He even asked to die!

These faithful servants of God did not sanitize their complaints. They simply bared their souls to Him. And for our sakes, He bared them to us. May it help us handle our pain as honestly as they did and know that it's okay. He is listening.

Praying in Hope

Father, I am so grateful that You can handle my raw self-honesty, even when it is ruthless. I don't want to come before You with any pretense. There is no reason for me to wear any masks. There is nothing I can hide from You! When I need to unleash my intense thoughts and emotions, please help me to follow Your way past them. Thank You for being my safe place. Thank You that I am secure in Your love, Your grace, Your mercy, and Your forgiveness. Thank You that You will never let me go. In Jesus' name, amen.

DAY

28

Wiping Away Your Tears

> God himself will be with them and be their God; he will wipe every tear from their eyes. Death will be no more; mourning and crying and pain will be no more.
>
> Revelation 21:3–4

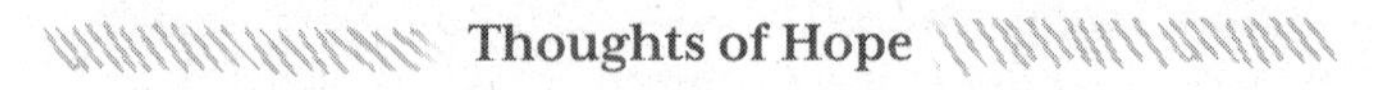

Thoughts of Hope

Are you sensing a greater need for time with God? Do you seem to get all your ducks in a row and then feel your broken places crying out afresh? The dichotomy is a human one to which any living soul can attest. Let it remind you of how much you need God. Don't worry; it's not a worrisome sign. It is simply an affirmation of your humanity that will help you stay honest before Him.

Twenty-first-century schedules are insane, and your time for morning devotions can seem hard-fought. Yet even your morning devotions cannot satisfy your need for God. Just look around you—brokenness is everywhere, in every person and situation. No one escapes it. What you need is not just a "word" to prime your motor each day. What you need and desire is the abiding presence and word of Christ, which cannot be reduced to a daily verse or a quick trip to the altar. Instead, it is an ongoing "Let it be" from the One who speaks continually.

How else can you recover from your sorrows? And who else can bring them out from your depths? Turn your attention to His "Let it be." Listen as it resounds, not only in the moment but across the landscape of your life. Let your heart absorb its sound and healing power, knowing that your need will follow you into eternity!

Beloved, the apostle John said that God will wipe away your tears on the other side of this life (see Revelation 21:4). That can mean only one thing: Your healing will not be complete in the moment of your passing. The more open you are to God's penetrating gaze, the more your unfinished business will be settled this side of death. But not everything will be settled here. When you leave this world, you will still need the Master's touch.

The hurts you didn't cry through, groan through, or agonize through in this life will rise to the surface in the open presence of Truth Himself. The wounds that remain will not bar you from the place of ultimate rejoicing. Nor will they dim the effulgence of His presence. Your remaining imperfections will not keep you from your eternal home or ward off the love and compassion of the God you will see face-to-face. The One who searches your heart and mind now will search them then. He will not say, "Thank heaven you made it," and overlook your residual brokenness. He will not retract His outstretched arm because you reached your destination.

The Father did not give His only Son just so you could join the celebration. No! When you cross over, the God of all compassion will finish the work He began in you (see Philippians 1:6). You did not join His club; you entered His abode, and there every tear will be addressed in the beauty of His holiness. Your disintegration and every vestige of sin will be set right. You will stand before the One who not only gives health and life but *is* health and life. And there, you will be made whole.

In the meantime, give yourself some of the grace He also gives. Accept yourself as a work in progress, a human being on an eternal journey in the forever company of your Maker. You might not be where you think you should be; but you are not where you once were. And where you are going is above and beyond all you can think or imagine.

Moving in Hope

Because we have been marked by what occurred in the Garden of Eden, you and I desperately need healing, salvation, deliverance, and love. Our need never lessens, and no one is exempt from it. We might try to navigate the world's corrupted currents in our strength or supposed expertise, but those waters are deeper and more powerful than we can master in this life. Only one man—the God-Man—could command those waters and even walk on them.

You and I can only acknowledge our fragmentation and accept it as part of the journey. When you cry your tears and groan your groans, do it with the understanding that a better day is ahead. In that day, the King Himself will receive you. And in eternity, He will wipe away any tears that remain. Only when He is finished will your deliverance be complete.

Praying in Hope

Father, I am becoming ever more mindful of what it means to allow all that is within me to bless Your holy name. "All" includes my negative and afflictive emotions; my fears, wounds, sorrows, and despairs; my heartaches and griefs. I have nothing to hide from You and no need to hold anything back. Your love will never let me go, and You have made room for me to be utterly transparent. Help me to hear Your "Let it be." Help me turn my pain into praise, my worries into worship, and my heartaches into hope. In Jesus' name, amen.

DAY

29

The Truth Prevails

Heal me, O Lord, and I shall be healed; save me, and I shall be saved, for you are my praise. See how they say to me, "Where is the word of the Lord? Let it come!"

Jeremiah 17:14–15

Thoughts of Hope

Beloved, when you find yourself in the deepest valley, your cries for the truth become more pronounced and pressing. As your sense of urgency increases, your patience becomes more strained, especially when the very thing you need most seems to be in the shortest supply. This conundrum is hardest to bear when you are suffering. Yet I can tell you what such seasons have taught me: Even if the truth doesn't prevail in this instant, it will prevail and not fail.

When hell itself seems to invade your life, the idea of waiting seems unjust. The powers of darkness may be hurling lies at you night and day—lies about God and about your standing with Him or lies about whether you will make it through your current difficulty. Their accusations are hurtful and cruel. In the onslaught, the truth can seem so distant and hidden as to be nonexistent. Your misery can threaten to overwhelm you, until you doubt your ability to stand. I know what that pressure is like. I know how defeated and alone you can feel. And I know that it is not the end of your story.

Notice what James says about those "who endure": "Indeed we count them blessed. . . . You have heard of the perseverance of Job and seen the end intended by the Lord—that the Lord is very compassionate and merciful" (James 5:11 NKJV). Job persevered, not because he was strong but because he trusted the One who is "very compassionate and merciful." James invites us to remember Job's stand and realize that transformation can take longer than we first hoped.

That probably isn't what you want to hear in a difficult moment. It wasn't for me. My friend Vinnie had to remind me countless times that "the eternal God is your refuge, and underneath are the everlasting arms. He will drive out your enemies before you, saying, 'Destroy them!'" (Deuteronomy 33:27 NIV). Impatient and distraught as I was, I knew those words were true. Deep down, I understood that God's goodness could not be worked into the depths of my being with a quick wave of the hand. It took more than that and required many moments of reminding myself that God would not leave me and had never abandoned me. He would see me through my ordeal, however long it took. He was doing a deep work in me, and I had to learn to abide patiently.

Learning that was a process all by itself! We live in an "instant" world in which *waiting* is a dirty word. We are accustomed to pressing computer keys and accessing reams of information in a split second. Instead of "wasting" time cooking, we order meals online and watch flickering icons that tell us our food is getting closer. We want everything *fast*.

If you need an ambulance, fast is the ticket. But fast is not always the right answer. Are you crying out for the truth this very minute? Are your nerves frayed and your hopes fading? Does the truth seem doomed? Maybe you have given up on it altogether, believing that the whole world has gone to hell in a handbasket and truth has left the planet. Let me be your Vinnie in this moment: When you persist in seeking the truth, you will come to *the* Truth. He is a Person, and He has not left the scene. You can be 100 percent certain that no matter how deep God's work in you goes, *the* Truth will prevail. In time, you will see "the end intended by the Lord" (James 5:11 NKJV). And it will have been worth the wait!

Moving in Hope

God is *for* you! The Truth is working in you and through you. The healing work of the cross is answering your cries and healing your fragmentation, even when you see no outward evidence. The fullness of your healing might not appear today or tomorrow, but that does not mean it isn't coming.

You and I think differently from God. He operates in the context of eternity. You and I are enslaved to the clock and can barely see into tomorrow. The work He is doing takes time and will continue after you cross the threshold into glory. For now, your part is to put one foot in front of the other and trust Him. Do that and you will be moving closer and closer to the fullness—the shalom—that God has promised. You can count on Him to prevail.

Praying in Hope

Father, I've read certain passages of Scripture again and again, never expecting to endure what they describe. Now it feels like I've been afflicted in every way. Remind me that I'm not crushed. I've been perplexed and feeling hemmed in; please keep me from despair. I've been struck down; please let me know that I'm not out for the count. If this is part of the dying of Jesus in me, then let the rising of new life in Jesus also be my portion. Grant me Your grace. Thank You that You hear me as I call out in hope, even against hope. In Jesus' name, amen.

DAY
30

This Too Shall Pass

Our slight, momentary affliction is producing for us an eternal weight of glory beyond all measure, because we look not at what can be seen but at what cannot be seen, for what can be seen is temporary, but what cannot be seen is eternal.

2 Corinthians 4:17–18

Thoughts of Hope

During your "momentary affliction," seeing past the moment is difficult. When every tick of the clock brings pain, the perspective of eternity requires more effort. It's no wonder Job's complaint to God began with a death wish! Job did not threaten suicide but essentially said, "If only I had died when I left my mother's womb!" He was so heartbroken that death looked better to him than life. It's easy to question his perspective. His "friends" did. But they were not in his shoes. Anyone who had experienced what Job suffered, or even honestly considered it, would surely have had compassion for Job.

Knowing a little about trauma and the human condition, I think even Job was terrified by the darkness of his thinking. He grappled with deep, existential fears and was at a complete loss to explain the tragedies that befell him. As if his setbacks were not unbearable enough, he became isolated in his suffering and utterly misunderstood. He was painted into a corner with no apparent way out.

Unless that kind of disaster has darkened your door, you cannot imagine what Job felt. But if you know, you know. Most people get a taste of intense pain at some point, as I did. The intensity of my suffering was real—*too real*. I was not suicidal, but I would not have minded one bit if God had chosen to quietly take me out. Anything seemed better than enduring another dark night. Yet by God's grace, I did what Job did each day: I took another step. My steps were feeble, but they were all I had. God knew that and met me right where I was.

Are you there, beloved? Are you wrestling day after day, horrified to find that death looks better to you than life? Do you fear that life will never be good again? Does there seem to be no way back from the brink? Even if you answered yes to these questions, there is more of life ahead. As extreme as your suffering might be, it is more common than you think. From your dark wood, it looks like everybody's life is rosy except yours. Other people seem to be doing the things that once delighted you but don't matter to you now. The truth is that not everyone comes to a crossroad at the same time. Nor can you compare what you feel on the inside to what other people seem to portray from the outside. *Everyone* deals with their own brand of pain in their own way and time.

The point is that you are not alone; you are human. It might seem that you are done for. It might be hard to imagine that you could ever recover from your ordeal. You might find it hard to see yourself enjoying life again or overcoming your present grief. That is part of being human: your present affliction appears to be the entirety of your existence. But there *is* life on the other side of your crisis, and there is *always* hope. Even Job came through his struggle and was more blessed than he had previously been. Yes, he suffered greatly, but he remained faithful. So did God, who vindicated Job and lifted him out of his devastation.

Your present distress and even your despair shall pass. God is leading you through your chaos and has yet to reveal the extent of all that He will accomplish through you. So walk on, beloved. Walk on!

Moving in Hope

When your life seems to crumble before your eyes, your thoughts can go to unexpected and alarming places. When they do, remember this crucial fact: *You are not your thoughts.* You need not fear your thoughts or deny them. It is far healthier to accept the fact that you have them. *But they are not you*. They are not your personality. They are your enemy, and accepting their existence is far different from adopting them.

Your thoughts may not be yours at all! Just because you hear them in your mind doesn't mean they came from you. So frustrate the enemy by refusing to own what he tries to deliver. He doesn't fight fair. But there is no fair fight when God is involved, is there?

Praying in Hope

Father, I thank You that I am not my thoughts, and I am not my feelings. I am learning that I have thoughts and feelings, but the deeper part of me is able to step back and observe them without judging them. Help me to step back in that way so I don't make my thoughts and feelings say more than they are really saying. Teach me to observe them and interpret them from a place of faith, hope, and love, knowing that You are making me an overcomer in Christ Jesus, and He is leading me to triumph! In His name, amen!

NOTES

Introduction

1. Dante Alighieri, *The Divine Comedy: Inferno*, canto I, trans. A. S. Kline, Poetry in Translation, accessed March 23, 2023, https://www.poetryintranslation.com/PITBR/Italian/DantInf1to7.php.

2. Alfred Korzybski, *Science and Sanity: An Introduction to Non-Aristotelian Systems and General Semantics*, 5th ed. (Brooklyn, NY: Institute of General Semantics, 1994), 61.

Day 1 Firmly on the Edge of Hope

1. The unconscious mind is "the region of the psyche containing memories, emotional conflicts, wishes, and repressed impulses that are not directly accessible to awareness but that have dynamic effects on thought and behavior." *APA Dictionary of Psychology*, s.v. "unconscious," accessed December 27, 2021, https://dictionary.apa.org/unconscious.

Day 8 Being with Your Pain

1. Teresa of Avila to Don Alvaro de Mendoza, Veas, May 11, 1575, ed. Dan Burke and Anthony Lilles, *30 Days with Teresa of Avila* (Steubenville, OH: Emmaus Road, 2015), Day 15, Kindle.

Day 10 Beauty for Ashes

1. John Newton, "Amazing Grace," 1779.

Day 12 Not Resignation but Acceptance

1. C. G. Jung, *Modern Man in Search of a Soul* (San Diego: Harvest, 1933), 234.

Day 13 Check Your Thoughts

1. *APA Dictionary of Psychology*, s.v. "cognitive distortion," accessed December 10, 2021, https://dictionary.apa.org/cognitive-distortion.

Day 14 What If?

1. Zia Sherrell, "What to Know About Existential Anxiety," Medical News Today, June 30, 2022, https://www.medicalnewstoday.com/articles/existential-anxiety.

Day 16 The Human Condition

1. Karl Albrecht, "The (Only) Five Fears We All Share," *Psychology Today*, March 22, 2012, https://www.psychologytoday.com/ca/blog/brainsnacks/201203/the-only-5-fears-we-all-share.

Dr. Mark Chironna is a lifelong learner who studies for the sake of his call: to serve Christ by bringing His saving, healing, and empowering truth to everyday people. All people are created in the image of God, yet everyone faces adversity, disappointment, and difficulty. Knowing this, Dr. Chironna preaches, teaches, speaks, and writes about the gospel and shares transparently about his own difficult seasons. He believes that to know and love Christ is to honor and understand not only the divine destiny of every human being but also the sufferings that are part of the human condition. Because of this, he labors to equip others. His hope is that Christ might be fully formed in them, for their benefit and God's glory.

Dr. Chironna holds a holistic view of spirituality, psychology, and theology. He does not see people as segmented beings but as integrated persons for whom the spiritual, physical, emotional, and psychological are inseparable. His view is not primarily philosophical but theological. He therefore emphasizes orthodoxy, sound teaching, and adherence to the Great Tradition that has guided the Church through the millennia. Dr. Chironna's extensive multidisciplinary training and experience includes board-certified coaching, a master's degree in psychology, a doctoral degree in applied semiotics and future leadership studies, and a PhD in theology from the University of Birmingham (UK). For Dr. Chironna, these endeavors are more than theoretical and academic; they are a practical part of his mission to serve others, and particularly the Body of Christ.

In addition to pastoring the flock at Church on the Living Edge in Orlando, Florida, Dr. Chironna is the presiding bishop of Legacy Edge Alliance, a worldwide fellowship of senior apostolic leaders and churches. He is also the bishop protector of the Order of St. Maximus the Confessor, an order recently inaugurated by the Charismatic Council of Bishops and devoted to the furthering of sound prophetic practice. His outreach includes a weekly television program, *On the Living Edge*, as well as *The Edge Podcast* and Facebook, Twitter, and Instagram platforms. Dr. Chironna and his wife, Pastor Ruth Chironna, have two grown sons and four grandchildren.

On the Living Edge, Daystar Television,
Thursdays, 10:30 p.m.

The Edge Podcast, available on all platforms

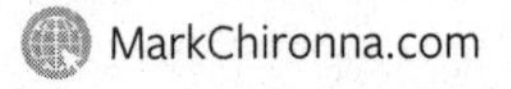